CAPTAIN SWORD & CAPTAIN PEN

*This special copy
is presented to you with our*

SEASON'S GREETINGS *&* BEST WISHES
FOR A HAPPY *&* PROSPEROUS
NEW YEAR

1   9   8   5

Blackwell North America, Inc.

LAKE OSWEGO, OREGON   ·   BLACKWOOD, NEW JERSEY

LEIGH HUNT
(1784-1859)

CAPTAIN SWORD
AND
CAPTAIN PEN

An Anti-War Poem
First Published in 1835
Here Reproduced in Facsimile
To Mark the Bicentennial of the
Author's Birth
With an Introduction to This Edition by

RHODES DUNLAP

Iowa City
FRIENDS OF THE
UNIVERSITY OF IOWA LIBRARIES

1984

Library of Congress Cataloging in Publication Data

Hunt, Leigh, 1784–1859.
    Captain Sword and Captain Pen.

    "First published in 1835 & here reproduced in
facsimile to mark the bicentennial of the author's birth"
    1. War poetry, English.   2. Protest poetry, English.
3. Peace–Poetry.   I. Dunlap, Rhodes.   II. Title.
PR4812.C3 1984   821'.7   83–25464
ISBN 0–087414–027–7

LEIGH HUNT
AND THE TWO CAPTAINS

The Background of a Poem

RHODES DUNLAP

When early in 1835 Leigh Hunt published *Captain Sword and Captain Pen*, his poetic protest against war, England was at peace, and the great powers had not fought one another since Wellington's famous victory at Waterloo in 1815. It would be almost another twenty years before their armies met again in the Crimean War. Not that the likelihood of war was ever remote; France remained a traditional enemy, and at the same time France was being replaced by an increasingly aggressive Russia as the nation most to be disliked and feared. British opinion was outraged by the brutality with which Russia put down a Polish revolt in 1830–1831, and a writer in the *Edinburgh Review* (April, 1832) declared, in terms to be heard again in our own century, that "two great antagonist principles now divide Europe – freedom and despotism." In 1834 the British Mediterranean Squadron had standing orders to help defend Constantinople in case of a Russian assault on that city.

We might expect the international situation to figure prominently in Hunt's poem, but it does not, though one of the writers he quotes in his prose Postscript mocks at Russian autocracy while advising against war with Russia. What may seem even more surprising, to anyone who looks at Hunt's other writing from this period, is the fact that he now produced such an impassioned work.

Since the spring of 1834 he had served as editor, and written most of the contents, of *Leigh Hunt's London Journal,* a resolutely non-controversial weekly which proclaimed at its masthead its purpose "to assist the enquiring, animate the struggling, and sympathize with all." In the issue of September 3, 1834 he went so far in universal sympathy as to admit:

> There is a noble as well as ignoble warfare, and the time for either, for aught we know, may not have gone by. We condemn none of the mysterious struggles of humanity, . . . some of them perhaps nobler and more necessary than our ceasing to struggle in that sort; on the contrary, in 'sympathising with all,' how can we leave them out? But, as far as our own system of action goes, we may be allowed . . . to confine ourselves to the hope of winning and persuading. There are green fields in the world, as well as fields of battle.

Briefly he harked back to his earlier days as a fiercely militant journalist:

> Of a truth, it would not be difficult for us, old soldiers as we are, and accustomed to rougher labours in former times, to summon up a little of our old battle-grip. . . . But *cui bono?* Where would be the good of it . . . ? . . . We are at peace with all. . . .

But so benign an attitude, as it turned out, could not be sustained. In the issue of March 4, 1835, he apologizes for not providing his customary leading article because he has been "busy with a new poem which he is about to publish, intitled 'Captain Sword and Captain Pen,'" and a week later he writes that it "will probably be out by the time this notice appears. The poem is partly political; and so far nothing further will be said of it in the *London Journal,* which the Editor is determined to keep sequestered and serene from all sound of trouble and controversy, however conscientiously executed."

Now fifty years old, he could claim a long and unblemished record as a battler for good causes. In his weekly paper *The Examiner,* which he founded in 1808 with his brother John as publisher, he had spoken out so boldly against public evils as to be repeatedly taken to court, and in 1812 he and John were condemned to a heavy fine and two years in jail on a charge of libeling the scandalous Prince Regent. He thus became a well-known public martyr, detested by many a Tory but much admired in liberal circles; and in succeeding years, though worldly prosperity eluded him, he unflaggingly built up moral capital. As a critic he boldly championed young poets who were deserving though as yet unknown, and in the political arena he was a tireless advocate of Parliamentary Reform. More than most men, he earned the right to take pleasure in a clear conscience – and to an unsympathetic eye he might seem annoyingly complacent. We glimpse Hunt late in 1832 in the diary of Sir Denis Le Marchant, at a gathering "at Lytton Bulwer's, the novelist": "Leigh Hunt's self importance was ludicrous – talking of the persecution he had suffered – he observed that it had had great results. It had, in conjunction with similar persecutions, been the great cause of reform. 'Yes, we worked this revolution. . . .'" (*Three Early Nineteenth Century Diaries,* ed. A. Aspinall, 1952, p. 278.) Le Marchant was secretary to Lord Brougham, to whom Hunt was to dedicate his anti-war poem in 1835, and he had no apparent reason to judge Hunt unfairly. But Shelley, many years before, was probably a more perceptive judge of Hunt's moral self-assurance; in a draft of his Preface to *Adonais* he wrote that, unlike poor Keats, who (as Shelley believed) was done to death by hostile critics, "my friend Hunt has a very hard skull to crack, and will take a deal of killing."

Composed with intense conviction, *Captain Sword and Captain Pen* has a double theme: the ugliness of war despite war's glamorous trappings, and the inevitable triumph of all that is noblest in the human spirit. Hunt wrote it while living at No. 4 (now No. 22) Upper Cheyne Row in Chelsea, near the Thames. He had brought his large family there in 1833, at a time when "our fortunes were at their worst, and my health almost of a piece with them." His health was to remain uncertain, and though by 1835 he had, as he said, a coat on his back so that he could again visit friends, by 1836 he was to find himself in danger of debtor's prison. But he was to remember with affection the "sense of quiet and repose" in the unpretentious house, where he set aside a small upstairs room as "a *sanctum,* into which no perturbation was to enter, except to calm itself with religious and cheerful thoughts (a room thus appropriated in a house appears to me an excellent thing)." In 1834 he acquired as neighbor Thomas Carlyle, whose *Sartor Resartus* had been appearing in *Fraser's Magazine* (being received there, according to the publisher, with "unqualified dissatisfaction"). Carlyle had corresponded with Hunt, and it was Hunt who found the nearby house for him, but, though Hunt was to quote Carlyle at length in the Postscript of his poem, their personal exchanges were less happy. In a letter of August 5, 1834, Carlyle writes of Hunt: "His way of thought and mine are utterly at variance; a thing which grieves him much, not me. He accounts for it by my 'Presbyterian upbringing,' which I tell him always I am everlastingly grateful for. He talks forever about 'happiness,' and seems to me the very miserablest man I ever sat and talked with."

Hunt's way of thought, which Carlyle elsewhere calls "innocent-hearted," might be described as consisting of variations on a single elementary theme – namely, our clear duty to fight evil and to keep faith in the ultimate triumph of good. These were tenets of what he called the Religion of the Heart. It was from an exalted sense of duty that he wrote *Captain Sword and Captain Pen;* if his clashes with Carlyle influenced the poem at all they must have acted as a stimulus to push forward with the writing. It was a painful duty because of the terrible events which, by the nature of his subject, he was required to make vivid – horrors from which the pages of *Leigh Hunt's London Journal*

were happily insulated. In his *Autobiography* he re-
calls: "I was several times forced to quit my task by
accesses of wonder and horror so overwhelming, as to
make me burst out in perspiration (a thing very difficult
in me to produce), and . . . nothing but the physical
relief thus afforded me, the early mother-taught lesson
of subjecting the one to the many, and perhaps the
habit of thinking the best in worst, and believing that
everything would, somehow or other, come right at
last, could have given me courage enough to face the
subject again." And he adds: "Men of action are too
apt to think that an author, and especially a poet,
dares and undergoes nothing as he peacefully sits by
his fireside 'indulging his muse.' But the muse is
sometimes an awful divinity."

In a sense Hunt had been preparing for many years
to write this poem. He says he was helped by having
once been a private in a regiment of volunteers which
was formed in expectation of a Napoleonic invasion,
and he associates some of the verses with his own
long hours on the parade-ground and at musket-drill:

> *"Steady, steady! – the masses of men*
> *Wheel, and fall in, and wheel again,*
> *Softly as circles drawn with pen.*

"I had been a part of the movement, and felt how soft
and orderly it was.

> *"Now for the flint, and the cartridge bite;*
> *Darkly gathers the breath of the fight,*
> *Salt to the palate, and stinging to sight.*

"Many a cartridge had I bitten, and thus learned the salt to that dreadful dinner."

For the most terrible aspects of battle he depended necessarily on the accounts of others, which he had clearly been accumulating for a long time. The earliest is the note which Robert Southey appended to his "Ode to Horror," a poem written in 1791 and printed in 1797; this note, quoted complete in Hunt's Post-script, "made such an impression on me in my youth, that I never afterwards could help calling it to mind when war was spoken of." Other harrowing details were based on published sources which in 1835 he did not think it necessary to quote directly. He was always moved to outrage at any example of cruelty or injustice, and in 1811 had been prosecuted for a pro-test against flogging in the army.

It was with a fine sense of appropriateness that Hunt placed on his title-page some lines from Milton's *Paradise Regained;* they form part of Christ's answer to Satan, who has tried to tempt him with earthly glory. When we look at Hunt's poetry chronologically, a pattern suggestive of the two Captains first emerges in the symbolic figures of False Glory and Real Glory in his masque *The Descent of Liberty,* which he wrote, while still in prison, to celebrate Napoleon's defeat and exile to Elba in 1814. The dramatic action shows the foiling of a Dark Enchanter and the subsequent bliss of the liberated victims as they pursue the arts of peace. Near the end there is a Vision of False Glory – "to the sound of trumpets and other warlike music . . .

a long train of laurelled soldiers, horse and foot. As they move onward, the word Slave is seen worked on their backs. To these . . . a number of painters, poets, and musicians, . . . but the same word is discovered on them. . . . Lastly, . . . the Conqueror dressed in purple, in a haughty attitude," but followed by a dark cloud behind which may be seen "several turbulent, weeping, and indignant shapes, representing the Passions, Misery, Widowhood, &c. . . . and the figure of Pity closing the whole." In contrast, the Vision of Real Glory shows a procession of sturdy countrymen with sheathed swords. "These are followed by poets, painters, and musicians, . . . wearing an air of frankness, and treading with a firm step." This time the Conqueror's chariot is followed by a snowy cloud behind which are "radiant angelic figures, Serenity, Happiness, &c., the whole concluding with the figure of Homage, bearing aloft a heart in his two hands, to which he looks upward with veneration." Unfortunately it was not long before Hunt saw that the defeat of Napoleon had brought to Europe not liberty but a restoration of the old autocracies. When Napoleon escaped from Elba and raised a new army, Hunt took the opportunity to reconsider his attitude, and in the *Examiner* of May 28, 1815, less than a month before the Battle of Waterloo, he announced that, "seeing how the Royal Liberators have just been acting, . . . we really believe we would manage to outlive the catastrophe" if Napoleon should emerge the victor.

But Hunt was never one to let disillusionment with

men or events make him change his principles, and twenty years later *Captain Sword and Captain Pen* shows these principles to be in no way shaken, though they receive a new topical application. In his preliminary "Advertisement" Hunt speaks of "a great public crisis"; this is not, as one might assume before reading further, a threat of war but a crisis in domestic politics, when the Whig ministry, which had secured passage of the great Parliamentary Reform Bill of 1832, was about to be replaced by the Tory ministry of Sir Robert Peel—a change which threatened to bring to power what in a footnote (p.33) Hunt calls "Military Toryism." This reference is made more explicit in Hunt's prose "Postscript; Containing Some Remarks on War and Military Statesmen." When the Whigs were dismissed in November 1834 the Duke of Wellington, the old hero of Waterloo and the most eminent of Tories (he had been Prime Minister in 1828–30), served as caretaker while Peel, the newly designated Prime Minister, rushed home from an Italian holiday. And though Peel was not himself a military man, Hunt was sure (p.75) that "notwithstanding his abilities" he would "turn out to be nothing but a servant of the aristocracy, and (more or less openly) of a barrack-master"—i.e., the Duke of Wellington. How little Hunt had his mind on a possible war with Russia is suggested by his rhetorical question (p. 81), "Do we want a soldier at the head of us, when there is nobody abroad to fight with?"

Toryism and militarism had long been linked in

Hunt's perceptions of evil. Though he says he does not like to indulge in personalities, he cannot help identifying, "in some measure, the Power of the Sword with several successive individuals, and with the Duke of Wellington most, because he is the reigning shape, and includes all its pretensions" (p. 90).

Arthur Wellesley, first Duke of Wellington (1769 – 1852), was thus cast in the role of Captain Sword. Lavishly honored and rewarded for his military successes climaxed by Waterloo, he had taken a significant part in restoring "legitimate" power in Europe. When he became Prime Minister in 1828, the *Examiner* – which, though no longer edited by Hunt, expressed dependably liberal views – jeered at what it considered his shortcomings, and offered for a start on his education a rhymed alphabet. "A," it begins, "is our 'ancient Ally' the Great Turk – / B is the Bigotry good for our work," and so on to "Z for the Zany who sits at the helm." Wellington took no notice of such attacks – to which, indeed, he should have been long inured. Many years earlier the true-blue Whig Byron had assailed him in *Don Juan* (ix.4):

> You are "the best of cut-throats": – do not start;
> The phrase is Shakespeare's, and not misapplied: –
> War's a brain-spattering, windpipe-slitting art,
> Unless her cause by Right be sanctified.
> If you have acted *once* a generous part,
> The World, not the World's masters, will decide;
> And I shall be delighted to learn who,
> Save you and yours, have gained by Waterloo?

10

Later in *Don Juan* (xi.83) Byron mused further on what he had seen in the seven years since 1815:

> I have seen Napoleon, who seem'd quite a Jupiter,
>   Shrink to a Saturn. I have seen a Duke
> (No matter which) turn politician stupider,
>   If that can well be, than his wooden look.

Both Hunt and Byron made satirical use – Hunt in a long poem called "The Dogs," Byron in a single line and footnote – of an incident related by a soldier who served (and nearly starved) under Wellington in Spain: five soldiers including himself had been assigned the duty of breaking biscuit "to make a mess for Lord Wellington's hounds. I was very hungry, and thought it a good job at the time, as we got our own fill while we broke the biscuit, – a thing I had not got for some days." Byron seems to have obtained the story from Hunt.

Wellington's deep-grained conservatism looked all the more formidable because of his obvious personal courage and sincerity, which Hunt was at pains to acknowledge. He had endured unflinchingly the unpopularity, and even some threats on his life, which resulted from his opposition to the Reform Bill; mobs twice broke the windows of Apsley House, his London residence, and he simply installed iron shutters. When the Chairman of the Birmingham Political Union threatened that if the Reform Bill did not pass he would lead a march on London, 200,000 strong, the Duke's response is said to have been, "Where are they going to get shoes?" The only good thing Hunt has to report of Captain Sword comes toward the end of the horror-filled Fourth Canto: when Captain Sword looks at the heaps of slain on the battlefield he "hasteth a tear from his old grey eye." The Duke of Wellington indeed wept after Waterloo. But if Captain Sword, in the prophecy which concludes Hunt's poem, "rusted apart," Wellington did not. Even by the time the poem was published in 1835 he had regained much of his popularity, and when he died in 1852 Tennyson, as Poet Laureate, could plausibly mourn him as "the last great Englishman."

As for Captain Pen, Hunt says nothing to identify him with any single person. Hunt's own long fights in Captain Pen's cause were waged as an individual only; he was himself no captain. But had he chosen to cast someone explicitly for the role, he might well have named his friend Henry Brougham (1778 – 1868), who was created Baron Brougham and Vaux in 1830 when he became Lord Chancellor in the Reform ministry. Apostle of peace, opponent of the slave trade, reformer of the courts and of education, founder (with others) of the University of London and of the Society for the Propagation of Useful Knowledge, admired speaker and writer on almost every subject under the sun, Brougham had served as legal counsel to the Hunts in their trials of 1811 and 1812, and thereafter had conducted a lively correspondence with Leigh Hunt on literary and other topics, including the evils of war ("I have been extremely occupied in the fight against arbitrary power in its two worst shapes – the military establishment and the Income Tax"). Brougham cast himself, if not as Captain Pen, as at least a herald of Captain Pen when on January 29, 1828 he defied Wellington, recently made Prime Minister, with a dramatically resonant speech in the House of Commons. Taking note of the supposedly widespread apprehension at Wellington's new power, he declared:

> I have no fear of slavery being introduced into this country by the sword. It would take a stronger man than the Duke of Wellington, though he be at once Prime Minister, and Commander-in-Chief of the Army; and though, added to the Army, he should have the Mitre [of the Archbishop of Canterbury], and to that the Great Seal [of the Lord Chancellor]. . . . These are not the times when the soldier only is abroad. Somebody of more importance has risen, who has reduced the soldier to nothing, even if he were ten thousand times more potent than he is. In the nineteenth century, new power bears sway: the Schoolmaster is abroad (*Hear, hear!*). I will trust more to him, armed with his primer, than to the soldier with his bayonet (*Hear, hear!*).

The comment of a writer in the *Examiner* was one which Hunt would have read with enthusiastic approval: "That word, 'the Schoolmaster is abroad' must strike terror to the heart, or some other quarter, of the Noble Duke. . . . There is no Army now like the Alphabet, no powder like the ink, no cannon like the grey goosequill." A speech which Brougham made seven years later, on laying the foundation-stone of the Mechanics' Institute in Liverpool on July 20, 1835, sounds as though the "Schoolmaster" theme had been given new life by a reading of Hunt's recently published poem. In the adulation with which the poem is dedicated to Brougham, Hunt says nothing which in 1835 was not literally true.

In any case, the poem and its Postscript make clear that neither Captain Pen nor Captain Sword can be completely or exclusively identified with any one person. Captain Sword is closely associated not only with Wellington and Peel but with two of Hunt's fellow-poets, Robert Southey and William Wordsworth. Southey had been a young radical but had changed his views and had been appointed Poet Laureate in 1813; early in 1835 Peel, as Tory Prime Minister, offered to make him a baronet. While Hunt had spent two years in jail for printing the truth of the Prince Regent, Southey thought the penalty not severe enough: "I have long wished that transportation were made the punishment for such offences. . . . It would remove the offenders out of the way of pity and of mischief, whereas in prison they contrive to excite both. Cobbett and Leigh Hunt were as mischievous in confinement as out of it." (Quoted by A. Aspinall, *Politics and the Press, c. 1870–1850*, 1947, p. 57n.) When in 1817 Southey issued a protest against the unauthorized publication of his early radical work *Wat Tyler*, Hunt pronounced him "a base and malignant Renegade" (*Examiner*, May 11, 1817) and held him up to savage ridicule. Perhaps memory of the *Wat Tyler* embarrassment made Hunt all the happier to quote in his

Postscript Southey's youthful note on the horrors of
war. Southey's later work included a highly successful
Life of Nelson, a *History of the Peninsular War,* and a
series of *Lives of the Admirals* which, in 1835, was still
in progress. Mention might also be made of *The Poet's
Pilgrimage to Waterloo: by Robert Southey, Esq.,
Poet Laureate,* 1816, a tribute to "Waterloo and Wel-
lington" which declares "the hopes of mankind" to be
fulfilled in the now triumphant British power "To do
the will and spread the word of Heaven." Hunt had
once considered Southey a friend. "We are always
disposed to quarrel with ourselves for quarrelling
with him, and yet we cannot help it, whenever we
come in contact with his writings." When the two
passed in the street without speaking, Hunt felt bad
about it until he picked up Southey's latest publication,
"and this at once put an end to our sentimentality"
(*Examiner,* May 18, 1817).

Hunt's Postscript dismisses Southey with a few
contemptuous words and reserves its detailed attack
for the "great poet" Wordsworth—a judgment which
Hunt would alter to "fine poet" when he republished
his comments. The lines to which he takes particular
exception, in which Wordsworth informs the Deity
that "Carnage is thy daughter," occur in a Thanks-
giving Ode written after the Battle of Waterloo, and
almost from their first publication had provoked pro-
test and satire. Shelley parodied them in *Peter Bell
the Third —*

15

> . . . Carnage and Slaughter,
> Thy niece and thy daughter . . .

and Byron quoted them in a footnote (*Don Juan*, viii.9), with the comment that "this is perhaps as pretty a pedigree for Murder as ever was found out by Garter King at Arms." Ultimately, in 1845, Wordsworth recast the offending lines so as to express what is practically the same idea in less provocative terms. But he never disavowed the prose note which he prefixed to his poem:

> . . . Nor is it at the expense of rational patriotism, or in disregard of sound philosophy, that I have given vent to feelings tending to encourage a martial spirit in the bosoms of my countrymen, at a time when there is a general outcry against the prevalence of these dispositions. . . .

And he goes on to say that

> no people ever was or can be, independent, free, or secure, much less great, in any sane application of the word, without a cultivation of military virtues.

Not that bloodshed is the less dreadful, as he makes clear in his sonnet "Upon Visiting the Field of Waterloo" –

> . . . we felt as men *should* feel
> With such vast hoards of hidden carnage near,
> And horror breathing from the silent ground!

Wordsworth took no public notice of Hunt's rebuke.

16

In subscribing to a collection of Hunt's poems in 1832 he had called Hunt "a Man of Genius and Talent," though he did not want the subscription to be interpreted as a "test of Opinion," and there is no evidence that he changed his mind.

Except for the now relapsed Southey, none of the writers that Hunt's Postscript quotes in behalf of Captain Pen is a poet. The first is the famous Utilitarian philosopher Jeremy Bentham, who had died in 1832. Bentham initiated a friendship with Hunt in the early days of the *Examiner* because he liked what he read there, and later he visited Hunt in prison. Hunt took his quotation from Bentham's posthumously published *Deontology,* which had received favorable mention in *Leigh Hunt's London Journal* for April 2, 1834, under the heading: "News for the Utilitarians. Mr. Bentham's testimony to the pleasures of imagination, and the duty of cultivating agreeable thoughts." But the quotation in the Postscript is obviously selected to lend authority to ideas which Hunt's poem presents about false glory and the certainty of human progress. The Bentham excerpt is followed by one from an article which Hunt's friend and critic Thomas Carlyle had published in the *Edinburgh Review* (March, 1831), and exalts the intellect as the saving force in human existence. Hunt sent a copy of the newly published *Captain Sword and Captain Pen* to Carlyle, who thanked him in a cordial note without commenting on the poem. The third quotation comes from a recent book by Sir Francis Head (1793 – 1875), and probably caught

Hunt's eye because of its tribute to the "little child" and the "Penny Magazine," though Head has an anecdote about a Russian nobleman which is in itself memorable. Head had been present at Waterloo and had won British and Prussian decorations; he could well fulfill Hunt's purpose of showing "the actual hold which these speculations have taken of the minds of practical men – of men out in the world, and even of *soldiers*."

Captain Sword and Captain Pen was published by Charles Knight, who was also the publisher of *Leigh Hunt's London Journal*. It is apparent that, though both publications found devoted readers, neither brought in much money, and at the end of 1835 *Leigh Hunt's London Journal* was abruptly terminated. Reviews of Hunt's poem were sparse and mixed, though there was strong praise in *The Examiner* (March 29, 1835):

> Its object is to show the extremest horrors of War. . . . We will only say on that point that the tragedy it displays would be too horrible, too nearly allied to the grossness of the shambles, but for the amazing effect with which a sentiment is breathed into it, elevating, in the midst of all, the human heart and its hopes, and such as could alone have rendered in that ghastly scene, such sufferings pathetic, and such struggles sublime. . . . Most sincerely do we . . . congratulate Mr Hunt's reappearance as the author of a volume worthy in all respects of his genius, and devoted to one of the noblest purposes that can engage humanity.

But Hunt's ideas would have found their most numerous audience among the already converted, when a large part of his prose Postscript was reprinted in the official quarterly of the Society for the Promotion of Permanent and Universal Peace (*The Herald of Peace* for April, May, and June, 1835, and continued in the following issue). Hunt himself was never a member of the Society, which had been founded in 1816, but he must have welcomed their support.

Hunt's biographer Edmund Blunden, who considers *Captain Sword and Captain Pen* one of the most remarkable of Hunt's poems, comments on the skill, suggestive of cinematography, with which Hunt tells his story in a succession of quickly flashed scenes. The illustrations, which enhance the vividness of the verses, were provided by Hunt's talented eldest son, Thornton, born in 1810. Thornton Hunt's original drawings for the illustrations are preserved in the Brewer – Leigh Hunt Collection, lacking only the ballroom scene for Canto III, and are executed in ink and wash with a delicacy which is given firmer outlines by the engraver, John Jackson. Perhaps Jackson was called upon for the engraving because he was already doing very good work for Charles Knight's *Penny Magazine*.

The first of the illustrations, used as a frontispiece and also reproduced on the front cover of the poem as published in 1835, summarizes the theme of war's grim actuality. It shows a cenotaph where a laurel-wreath standard rises above a circle of trumpets and banners; a female figure with averted face draws back a curtain, and a male figure (perhaps the poet) points to a soldier who is revealed lying slain with a sword through his heart.

In contrast, the First Canto introduces Captain Sword and his forces in verse and picture at their most attractive. It might well be considered alongside Hunt's essay "A Battle of Ants" (*The Companion,* July 16, 1828; republished 1834). He had come across a magazine account of fighting ants, and, while he prepared to ponder the instincts of "the little Wellingtons and Napoleons," he saw passing at his window

> a troop of horse; a set of gallant fellows, on animals almost as noble, the band playing, and colours flying; . . . a progress of human hearts and thick-coming, trampling hoofs; a crowd of wills, composed into order and beauty by the will of another; ready death in the most gallant shape of life; self-sacrifice, taking out its holiday of admiration. . . . Was it all this? or was it nothing but a set of more imposing animals, led by others almost half as thoughtless? . . . The sight of one of these military shows is, to us, the most elevating and the most humiliating thing in the world. . . . One field, after a battle, with the cries of the wounded and the dying, . . . and the . . . dreadful lingering (perhaps on a winter's night), . . . is sufficient to do away all shallow and blustering attempts to make us take the shew of it for the substance.

In Canto Two, on the "Great Victory," Thornton Hunt's illustration shows the terrible reality of the fight, with horsemen attacking a line of foot soldiers and the victims beginning to go down. Many of the details in the narrative, such as the stench of blood, derive from contemporary accounts of Waterloo, though according to Hunt's notes in the 1849 edition there is one non-literary source: "The circumstance of 'lolling the tongues out,' during a charge of bayonets, on a hot and exhausting day, was told me in my youth, on the authority of a soldier who had served in Holland."

Canto Three is illustrated with an ironically charming picture of a victory ball. Hunt loved ballroom dancing as much as he did parades and pageantry. *Leigh Hunt's London Journal* on September 10, 1834, devotes four and a-half columns to an article on "Dancing and Dancers" ("Why do not people oftener get up dances at home . . . ? It would be a great addition to the cheerfulness and health of families"), and later issues follow up the topic. Hunt's ballroom repertory includes the old-fashioned minuet (popular in his earliest youth) and the country dance (also known as the Roger de Coverley and, in America, the Virginia reel), along with the waltz (thought daring because of the embrace of the dancers) and the galopade, a recent import from Hungary.

In Canto Four the scene shifts once more from the victory ball to the "Dance of Death" on the field after the battle, with its dead, its dying, and its unspeakable scavengers; the illustration shows a nude apocalyptic figure with a trumpet against a background of dark shapes. Again Hunt draws upon printed accounts, mostly of Waterloo and the Peninsular War – the latter for two of the most harrowing episodes: the wounded soldier ("this coal") burned in a grass fire, whose only hope is that the robbers roaming the field may kill him and thus end his suffering ("For gold he possesseth, and Murder is nigh!"), and – at the end of the canto –

the sack of a captured city, something of which both the French and the English had been guilty. There had been particularly gruesome accounts of the looting of San Sebastian by Wellington's forces despite the strict orders of their commander.

In Canto Five the destined defeat of Captain Sword begins with the American and French Revolutions and continues with the "Glorious Three Days" – the July Revolution which, in 1830, deposed King Charles X, last of the Bourbon rulers of France. In claiming to be not only Pitt and Lord Grey – two outstanding former prime ministers – but also Captain Pen himself, Captain Sword may refer to the Tory claim of being the true reformers (*The Examiner* on March 8, 1835 derides "the pretence of the Tory Ministry that it is big with reform"), but his coming "with gowned men" seems to glance more specifically at Wellington's being made Chancellor of Oxford University in 1834. The great Duke, to do him justice, had not been eager for this academic eminence, protesting that he possessed only a schoolboy's knowledge of Latin and Greek, but Oxford received him with wild acclaim. "Tories and true men," shouted the undergraduates. In the illustration Captain Sword holds up a pen in his right hand (his left being still on his sword in its scabbard) while he addresses a crowd of humble folk, one of whom holds a spade. On the interpretation here suggested, one would like to believe that the young man pointing to the Captain is an Oxford student and the gowned figures behind him Oxford dons, but the gowns do not look much like academic robes, and perhaps Thornton Hunt had a different symbolism in mind. Whether or not associated with Oxford, the gowned men could quite well be identified as the thinkers and scholars who have advanced the good of mankind. In one detail, the Captain's plumed hat, the illustration clearly disregards the text, which describes the professedly transformed Captain as "hatless."

Canto Six concludes the story with the steady march of progress that ensures the triumph of Captain Pen. In the illustration Captain Sword leans dejectedly against a wall, duly rusting, while his former soldiers, still in uniform, hail the messianically bright figure of Captain Pen. Among the wonders ready to serve Captain Pen is

> A creature . . .
> Half iron, half vapour, a dread to behold –
> Which evermore panted and evermore roll'd,
> And uttered his words a million fold.

Modern readers may not at once recognize this as the steam printing press, or "printing machine," invented in the first decade of the nineteenth century. When it was put to use in printing the *Times*, on November 29, 1814, that paper proclaimed: "Our Journal of this day presents to the public the practical result of the greatest improvement connected with printing, since the discovery of the art itself. . . . A system of machinery almost organic has been devised and arranged, which, while it relieves the human frame of its most laborious efforts in printing, far exceeds all human powers in rapidity and despatch." Hunt's poem was itself printed in 1835 on the steam press of C. and W. Reynell.

The final illustration, at the end of Hunt's volume, shows a happy family in the ideal new world – the gowned father with the youngest child at his knee, two older children paying dutiful respect, and the mother taking down a volume from the well-filled bookshelf.

In the Preface of the 1849 edition, Hunt said that he considered *Captain Sword and Captain Pen,* "in regard to expression, as one of the least faulty" of his writings. He felt special satisfaction with the meter, in which, instead of imitating the pentameter couplets of Dryden which had been his early model, he followed what he called elsewhere the "beautiful freedom" that Coleridge had demonstrated in the flexible four-beat line of "Christabel" – "calling to mind the liberties allowed to its old musical professors the minstrels" (*Imagination and Fancy,* 1844, p. 55). As for what the verses have to express, Louis Landré, in his two-volume study *Leigh Hunt,* thinks that the poem, despite its "tableaux riches et évocateurs," is flawed by its "banal" subject. It must be admitted that poets have deplored the miseries of war ever since Homer, and the idea that the pen is mightier than the sword is also centuries-old, though the wording by which it is now best known owes its currency to its use in Bulwer-Lytton's popular play *Richelieu,* produced in 1839. By Hunt's standards the potential banality of his theme would be inconsequential in the face of its truth. "Truth, of any great kind whatsoever, makes great writing" (*Imagination and Fancy,* p. 64), and there could be no mistaking his intention to present the truth about war freed of all false appearances. In the Preface to his 1832 *Poetical Works* he writes, "If there is no truth in my verses, I look for no indulgence."

After the poem was published in 1835, he would still not be done with it. In the Preface of the Third Edition, 1849, he says that for a second edition he had "omitted the worst part of the horrors which the poem itself contained"; no copy of a separately printed second edition appears to exist, and Charles Knight, in granting permission to print the poem in Hunt's *Poetical Works,* 1844, seems not aware of any second edition. Knight's letter is in the Brewer – Leigh Hunt Collection, fMS/H94ag.

Ludgate St January 17, 1844.

My dear Hunt/

> You are most freely welcome to the use of the Sword and Pen in the now proposed, or any future edition of your Poems. I sincerely trust that collected with the other charming things for which the world is your debtor, it may have a success which its first publication did not command, but which it so well deserved. In haste,

Ever truly yours

Chas Knight

Perhaps the cut version included in the 1844 collection amounted in Hunt's mind to a second edition. The deletions included not only the episodes which Hunt found most painful but also his anguished asides to the reader, which had been printed in 1835 in square brackets. In his 1844 Preface he says that the full horrors could be safely omitted because "the progress of mechanical science and its fusion of nations one with another . . . will . . . render war as absurd and impossible by-and-by, as it would be for Manchester to fight with Birmingham." Apparently he has in mind here the development of rapid steam transport; the first railway had begun service in 1825, and in 1838 the steamship *Great Western* crossed the Atlantic in fifteen days. Thus only enough unpleasant detail need be retained in the poem "to give entireness to the subject, and a due contrasting effect to the blessings of the growth of knowledge and good-will." He does not say, but he may have felt, that the poem is actually improved imaginatively when freed of authorial intrusions and reduplicated horrors. In 1838, fresh from reading *Oliver Twist* and part of *Nicholas Nickleby*, he had written to Dickens that "I think you sometimes push the terrible too far" (*Letters of Charles Dickens*, Clarendon Press, 1965, I, p. 686).

The Third Edition, 1849, completely reversed matters once more. Losing patience with "those who maintain that everybody is agreed respecting the horrors of war," and who thereupon try to shift the subject, he restored all his previous deletions and added notes which quote at length the war narratives from which the horrors of the poem are taken. He retained his 1835 Postscript under the heading "On the Duty of Considering the Horrors and the Alleged Necessity of War," though he cut out eleven paragraphs on the political crisis of 1834 – 35, and he swelled the amount of prose with further discourses which took cognizance for the first time of the progress achieved by Peace Societies in England and elsewhere, with strong voices increasingly heard in support. In 1838 Emerson had declared, in a Boston lecture sponsored by the American Peace Society, that "war is on its last legs," and Victor Hugo was to be the eloquent chairman of a Peace Congress at Paris in August, 1849. Seeking a publisher, Hunt asked the noted reformer John Bright whether the London Peace Society might undertake a new edition of his anti-war poem. On July 27, 1849, Bright replied:

> My friend Charles Gilpin of 5 Bishopsgate St Without is a publisher, & a leading friend of the peace movement, & I have seen him on the subject of your letters to me. He says the peace Comttee are short of funds, as all active & hard working societies usually are, and that they are too much pressed in other directions to be able to do anything with the publication of your work. I suggested to him that he might try the speculation himself

—whereupon Gilpin made a proposal to publish the poem which Bright advised Hunt to accept. "You will find him a most honorable man" (British Library, Ms. Addit. 38110). *Captain Sword and Captain Pen* accordingly appeared in its Third Edition with Gilpin's imprint; it received extended notice in *The Herald of*

Peace (January, 1850: "one of the noblest poetical protests ever uttered against the sinister idolatry of brute force") and *The Examiner* (June 1, 1850). Gilpin's list already included a *Peace Reading-Book* in which one finds Southey's "The Battle of Blenheim" (perhaps the most successful of all anti-war poems) but regrettably nothing by Hunt.

For the new edition Thornton Hunt's illustrations were not used, though the engravings seem to have been still available. When Hunt, even before the arrangement with Gilpin, asked Charles Knight for permission to republish the poem separately, Knight agreed on February 21, 1849, and added: "There are some wood-cuts, if I recollect rightly. I dare say they can be found, and if they will be of any use to you I shall be quite ready to hand you over this material property along with that subtle and ethereal thing called copyright" (Brewer – Leigh Hunt Collection, fMS/H94ag). But the Third Edition carried no illustrations; and when, in 1860, a year after Hunt's death, Thornton Hunt edited his father's collected poems, the illustrations – including one for *Captain Sword and Captain Pen* – were the work of the then prominent artist Edward Henry Corbould.

Besides the omission of Thornton Hunt's illustrations in 1849 another omission demands notice: Hunt withdrew the Dedication of the poem to Brougham.

After ceasing to be Lord Chancellor in 1834, Brougham had never held a post in any ministry; he was perceived as politically unreliable. But he continued to pursue a multitude of interests and to dazzle with his oratory. One of his supreme successes came at a festival held in Dover in honor of Wellington on August 30, 1839, where he proposed the great Duke's health in "a Speech which electrified its hearers, and which, diffused by the press, created scarcely less an effect upon its readers." In this speech Brougham, whose past political opposition to Wellington emphasized the non-partisan nature of his tribute, hailed "the Mighty Captain, who never advanced but to cover his arms with glory – the mightier Captain, who never retreated but to eclipse that glory by the far higher fame of . . . a moral courage which nothing can shake. . . . Our Hero has never drawn his sword but in that defensive war, which alone, of all warfare, is not the greatest of crimes." The distinction about defensive war seems to have been easily forgotten, for within the next decade Brougham was praising Austrian victories in Italy and Russian intervention to suppress a Hungarian revolt against the Hapsburgs. So erratic were his shifting commitments – and not only about war – that he became a favorite target of witty sallies in *Punch,* where one full-page cartoon shows him standing on his head, while in some deft verses he is the "learned lord"

> Who'd rather mount the mountebank's stage than be laid
> on the shelf,
> Who does with ease the difficult task of turning his back
> on himself.

Certainly he turned his back on what Hunt had once

expected him to stand for. On February 2, 1849, Queen Victoria's Speech from the Throne expressed a hope for continued peace and a consequent reduction in military expenditures; whereupon Brougham rose to say (as summarized in the *Annual Register*) that he

> doubted the good faith of those who insisted on the reduction of the Army and Navy. His noble and illustrious friend the Duke of Wellington always desired to reduce the Army to the smallest possible limits that were necessary for the defence of our honour and our possessions. . . . Since the last meeting of Parliament there was every reason to feel that the defences of the country ought to be strengthened. . . . England was especially bound not to forget her ancient alliance with Austria. . . . There was also that other great empire—Russia—the impregnable position of which formed a most valuable counterpoise to the dissemination of Republican doctrines.

Later in the year Brougham announced that he had been invited to participate in the forthcoming Peace Congress at Paris, but had declined the invitation.

Hunt handled the defection with dignity. Instead of a Dedication he inserted the following statement:

> One word more. The first and second editions of the poem were dedicated to a noble and learned Lord, for whom the writer has never ceased to entertain great and grateful respect; but as his lordship's opinions on the subject appear to have undergone some modifications that might have rendered the address to him not so proper, I have done what I thought least unbecoming to the space which it occupied, by leaving it unappropriated to anybody.

October 12th, 1849   LEIGH HUNT.

Brougham's changed views presented no threat to Hunt's own persistence. They may provide, rather, one reason for the uncompromising nature of his Third Edition. Though Captain Pen (or at least an imperfect human embodiment) turned out to be a lost leader, Leigh Hunt would, as Shelley had said, take a deal of killing.

The University of Iowa

September, 1983

The following is a facsimile of the first edition of *Captain Sword and Captain Pen,* 1835, made from a copy (828/H941c/cop 2) in the Brewer – Leigh Hunt Collection at The University of Iowa.

To

Marriott Smut

from his affectionate uncle.

CAPTAIN SWORD

AND

CAPTAIN PEN.

[*To face the Title.*

CAPTAIN SWORD AND CAPTAIN PEN.

𝔄 Poem.

BY LEIGH HUNT.

WITH SOME REMARKS ON

WAR AND MILITARY STATESMEN.

— If there be in glory aught of good,
It may by means far different be attained,
Without ambition, war, or violence.—MILTON.

LONDON:

CHARLES KNIGHT, LUDGATE STREET.

1835.

LONDON:

Printed by C. and W. REYNELL,
Little Pulteney Street.

ADVERTISEMENT.

This Poem is the result of a sense of duty, which has taken the Author from quieter studies during a great public crisis. He obeyed the impulse with joy, because it took the shape of verse; but with more pain, on some accounts, than he chooses to express. However, he has done what he conceived himself bound to do; and if every zealous lover of his species were to express his feelings in like manner, to the best of his ability, individual opinions, little in

themselves, would soon amount to an over-
whelming authority, and hasten the day of rea-
son and beneficence.

The measure is regular with an irregular
aspect,—four accents in a verse,—like that of
Christabel, or some of the poems of Sir Walter
Scott :

> Càptain Swòrd got ùp one dày—
> And the flàg full of hònour, as thòugh it could feèl—

He mentions this, not, of course, for readers
in general, but for the sake of those daily
acceders to the list of the reading public, whose
knowledge of books is not yet equal to their
love of them.

STEPPING IN MUSIC AND THUNDER SWEET,
WHICH HIS DRUMS SENT BEFORE HIM INTO THE STREET.

Canto 1. *p.* 1.

CAPTAIN SWORD AND CAPTAIN PEN.

I.

How Captain Sword marched to War.

Captain Sword got up one day,
Over the hills to march away,
Over the hills and through the towns,
They heard him coming across the downs,
Stepping in music and thunder sweet,
Which his drums sent before him into the street.
And lo! 'twas a beautiful sight in the sun;
For first came his foot, all marching like one,
With tranquil faces, and bristling steel,

B

And the flag full of honour as though it could feel,
And the officers gentle, the sword that hold
'Gainst the shoulder heavy with trembling gold,
And the massy tread, that in passing is heard,
Though the drums and the music say never a word.

And then came his horse, a clustering sound
Of shapely potency, forward bound,
Glossy black steeds, and riders tall,
Rank after rank, each looking like all,
Midst moving repose and a threatening charm,
With mortal sharpness at each right arm,
And hues that painters and ladies love,
And ever the small flag blush'd above.

And ever and anon the kettle-drums beat
Hasty power midst order meet;

And ever and anon the drums and fifes

Came like ˌmotion's voice, and life's;

Or into the golden grandeurs fell

Of deeper instruments, mingling well,

Burdens of beauty for winds to bear;

And the cymbals kiss'd in the shining air,

And the trumpets their visible voices rear'd,

Each looking forth with its tapestried beard,

Bidding the heavens and earth make way

For Captain Sword and his battle-array.

He, nevertheless, rode indifferent-eyed,

As if pomp were a toy to his manly pride,

Whilst the ladies lov'd him the more for his scorn,

And thought him the noblest man ever was born,

And tears came into the bravest eyes,

And hearts swell'd after him double their size,

And all that was weak, and all that was strong,
Seem'd to think wrong's self in him could not be wrong;
Such love, though with bosom about to be gored,
Did sympathy get for brave Captain Sword.

　So, half that night, as he stopp'd in the town,
'Twas all one dance, going merrily down,
With lights in windows and love in eyes,
And a constant feeling of sweet surprise;
But all the next morning 'twas tears and sighs;
For the sound of his drums grew less and less,
Walking like carelessness off from distress;
And Captain Sword. went whistling gay,
" Over the hills and far away. "

II.

How Captain Sword won a Great Victory.

Through fair and through foul went Captain Sword,

Pacer of highway and piercer of ford,

Steady of face in rain or sun,

He and his merry men, all as one;

Till they came to a place, where in battle-array

Stood thousands of faces, firm as they,

Waiting to see which could best maintain

Bloody argument, lords of pain;

And down the throats of their fellow-men

Thrust the draught never drunk again.

It was a spot of rural peace,
Ripening with the year's increase
And singing in the sun with birds,
Like a maiden with happy words —
With happy words which she scarcely hears
In her own contented ears,
Such abundance feeleth she
Of all comfort carelessly,
Throwing round her, as she goes,
Sweet half-thoughts on lily and rose,
Nor guesseth what will soon arouse
All ears — that murder's in the house ;
And that, in some strange wrong of brain,
Her father hath her mother slain.

Steady ! steady ! The masses of men
Wheel, and fall in, and wheel again,
Softly as circles drawn with pen.

Then a gaze there was, and valour, and fear,

And the jest that died in the jester's ear,

And preparation, noble to see,

Of all-accepting mortality ;

Tranquil Necessity gracing Force ;

And the trumpets danc'd with the stirring horse ;

And lordly voices, here and there,

Call'd to war through the gentle air ;

When suddenly, with its voice of doom,

Spoke the cannon 'twixt glare and gloom,

Making wider the dreadful room :

On the faces of nations round

Fell the shadow of that sound.

Death for death ! The storm begins ;

Rush the drums in a torrent of dins ;

Crash the muskets, gash the swords ;

Shoes grow red in a thousand fords;
Now for the flint, and the cartridge bite;
Darkly gathers the breath of the fight,
Salt to the palate and stinging to sight;
Muskets are pointed they scarce know where,
No matter: Murder is cluttering there.
Reel the hollows: close up! close up!
Death feeds thick, and his food is his cup.
Down go bodies, snap burst eyes;
Trod on the ground are tender cries;
Brains are dash'd against plashing ears;
Hah! no time has battle for tears;
Cursing helps better—cursing, that goes
Slipping through friends' blood, athirst for foes'.
What have soldiers with tears to do?—
We, who this mad-house must now go through,
This twenty-fold Bedlam, let loose with knives—

DOWN GO BODIES—SNAP BURST EYES—
TROD ON THE GROUND ARE TENDER CRIES.

Canto II. p. 8.

To murder, and stab, and grow liquid with lives —
Gasping, staring, treading red mud,
Till the drunkenness' self makes us steady of blood ?

[Oh ! shrink not thou, reader ! Thy part's in it too ;
Has not thy praise made the thing they go through
Shocking to read of, but noble to do ?]

No time to be " breather of thoughtful breath "
Has the giver and taker of dreadful death.
See where comes the horse-tempest again,
Visible earthquake, bloody of mane !
Part are upon us, with edges of pain ;
Part burst, riderless, over the plain,
Crashing their spurs, and twice slaying the slain.
See, by the living God ! see those foot
Charging down hill — hot, hurried, and mute !

They loll their tongues out ! Ah-hah ! pell-mell !
Horses roll in a human hell ;
Horse and man they climb one another —
Which is the beast, and which is the brother ?
Mangling, stifling, stopping shrieks
With the tread of torn-out cheeks,
Drinking each other's bloody breath —
Here's the fleshliest feast of Death.
An odour, as of a slaughter-house,
The distant raven's dark eye bows.

   Victory ! victory ! Man flies man ;
Cannibal patience hath done what it can —
Carv'd, and been carv'd, drunk the drinkers down,
And now there is one that hath won the crown :
One pale visage stands lord of the board —
Joy to the trumpets of Captain Sword !

His trumpets blow strength, his trumpets neigh,
They and his horse, and waft him away ;
They and his foot, with a tir'd proud flow,
Tatter'd escapers and givers of woe.
Open, ye cities ! Hats off ! hold breath !
To see the man who has been with Death ;
To see the man who determineth right
By the virtue-perplexing virtue of might.
Sudden before him have ceas'd the drums,
And lo ! in the air of empire he comes !

All things present, in earth and sky,
Seem to look at his looking eye.

III.

But Captain Sword was a man among men,
And he hath become their playmate again:
Boot, nor sword, nor stern look hath he,
But holdeth the hand of a fair ladye,
And floweth the dance a palace within,
Half the night, to a golden din,
Midst lights in windows and love in eyes,
And a constant feeling of sweet surprise;
And ever the look of Captain Sword
Is the look that's thank'd, and the look that's ador'd.

There was the country-dance, small of taste;

And the waltz, that loveth the lady's waist;

And the galopade, strange agreeable tramp,

Made of a scrape, a hobble, and stamp;

And the high-stepping minuet, face to face,

Mutual worship of conscious grace;

And all the shapes in which beauty goes

Weaving motion with blithe repose.

And then a table a feast displayed,

Like a garden of light without a shade,

All of gold, and flowers, and sweets,

With wines of old church-lands, and sylvan meats,

Food that maketh the blood feel choice;

Yet all the face of the feast, and the voice,

And heart, still turn'd to the head of the board;

THERE WAS THE COUNTRY DANCE, SMALL OF TASTE;
AND THE WALTZ, THAT LOVETH THE LADY'S WAIST.

Canto III. *p.* 14.

For ever the look of Captain Sword
Is the look that's thank'd, and the look that's ador'd.

Well content was Captain Sword ;
At his feet all wealth was pour'd ;
On his head all glory set;
For his ease all comfort met ;
And around him seem'd entwin'd
All the arms of womankind.

And when he had taken his fill
Thus, of all that pampereth will,
In his down he sunk to rest,
Clasp'd in dreams of all its best.

IV.

On What took place on the Field of Battle the Night after the Victory.

'Tis a wild night out of doors;
The wind is mad upon the moors,
And comes into the rocking town,
Stabbing all things, up and down,
And then there is a weeping rain
Huddling 'gainst the window-pane,
And good men bless themselves in bed;
The mother brings her infant's head
Closer, with a joy like tears,
And thinks of angels in her prayers;
Then sleeps, with his small hand in hers.

Two loving women, lingering yet
Ere the fire is out, are met,
Talking sweetly, time-beguil'd,
One of her bridegroom, one her child,
The bridegroom he. They have receiv'd
Happy letters, more believ'd
For public news, and feel the bliss
The heavenlier on a night like this.
They think him hous'd, they think him blest,
Curtain'd in the core of rest,
Danger distant, all good near;
Why hath their " Good night " a tear?

Behold him! By a ditch he lies
Clutching the wet earth, his eyes
Beginning to be mad. In vain
His tongue still thirsts to lick the rain,

That mock'd but now his homeward tears;
And ever and anon he rears
His legs and knees with all their strength,
And then as strongly thrusts at length.
Rais'd, or stretch'd, he cannot bear
The wound that girds him, weltering there:
And " Water ! " he cries, with moonward stare.

["I will not read it!" with a start,
Burning cries some honest heart;
"I will not read it ! Why endure
" Pangs which horror cannot cure ?
" Why — Oh why ? and rob the brave
" And the bereav'd of all they crave,
" A little hope to gild the grave ? "

Ask'st thou why, thou honest heart?
'Tis *because* thou dost ask, and *because* thou dost start.
'Tis because thine own praise and fond outward thought
Have aided the shews which this sorrow have wrought.]

A wound unutterable — Oh God!
Mingles his being with the sod.

["I'll read no more." — Thou must, thou must:
In thine own pang doth wisdom trust.]

His nails are in earth, his eyes in air,
And "Water!" he crieth — he may not forbear.
Brave and good was he, yet now he dreams
The moon looks cruel; and he blasphemes.

["No more! no more!" Nay, this is but one;

Were the whole tale told, it would not be done

From wonderful setting to rising sun.

But God's good time is at hand—be calm,

Thou reader! and steep thee in all thy balm

Of tears or patience, of thought or good will,

For the field—the field awaiteth us still.]

"Water! water!" all over the field:

To nothing but Death will that wound-voice yield.

One, as he crieth, is sitting half bent;

What holds he so close?—his body is rent.

Another is mouthless, with eyes on cheek;

Unto the raven he may not speak.

One would fain kill him; and one half round

The place where he writhes, hath up beaten the ground.

Like a mad horse hath he beaten the ground,

And the feathers and music that litter it round,

The gore, and the mud, and the golden sound.

Come hither, ye cities! ye ball-rooms, take breath!

See what a floor hath the dance of death!

   The floor is alive, though the lights are out;

What are those dark shapes, flitting about?

Flitting about, yet no ravens they,

Not foes, yet not friends—mute creatures of prey;

Their prey is lucre, their claws a knife,

Some say they take the beseeching life.

Horrible pity is theirs for despair,

And they the love-sacred limbs leave bare.

Love will come to-morrow, and sadness,

Patient for the fear of madness,

And shut its eyes for cruelty,

So many pale beds to see.

COME HITHER, YE CITIES! YE BALL-ROOMS TAKE BREATH!
SEE WHAT A FLOOR HATH THE DANCE OF DEATH.

Canto IV. *p.* 22.

Turn away, thou Love, and weep
No more in covering his last sleep ;
Thou hast him—blessed is thine eye !
Friendless Famine has yet to die.

A shriek !—Great God ! what superhuman
Peal was that ?   Not man, nor woman,
Nor twenty madmen, crush'd, could wreak
Their soul in such a ponderous shriek.
Dumbly, for an instant, stares
The field ; and creep men's dying hairs.

O friend of man ! O noble creature !
Patient and brave, and mild by nature,
Mild by nature, and mute as mild,
Why brings he to these passes wild

Thee, gentle horse, thou shape of beauty?
Could he not do his dreadful duty,
(If duty it be, which seems mad folly)
Nor link thee to his melancholy?

Two noble steeds lay side by side,
One cropp'd the meek grass ere it died;
Pang-struck it struck t' other, already torn,
And out of its bowels that shriek was born.

Now see what crawleth, well as it may,
Out of the ditch, and looketh that way.
What horror all black, in the sick moonlight,
Kneeling, half human, a burdensome sight;
Loathly and liquid, as fly from a dish;
Speak, Horror! thou, for it withereth flesh.

" The grass caught fire; the wounded were by;
Writhing till eve did a remnant lie;
Then feebly this coal abateth his cry;
But he hopeth! he hopeth! joy lighteth his eye,
For gold he possesseth, and Murder is nigh!"

O goodness in horror! O ill not all ill!
In the worst of the worst may be fierce Hope still.
To-morrow with dawn will come many a wain,
And bear away loads of human pain,
Piles of pale beds for the 'spitals; but some
Again will awake in home-mornings, and some,
Dull herds of the war, again follow the drum.
From others, faint blood shall in families flow,
With wonder at life, and young oldness in woe,
Yet hence may the movers of great earth grow.
Now, even now, I hear them at hand,

Though again Captain Sword is up in the land,

Marching anew for more fields like these

In the health of his flag in the morning breeze.

Sneereth the trumpet, and stampeth the drum,

And again Captain Sword in his pride doth come;

He passeth the fields where his friends lie lorn,

Feeding the flowers and the feeding corn,

Where under the sunshine cold they lie,

And he hasteth a tear from his old grey eye.

Small thinking is his but of work to be done,

And onward he marcheth, using the sun:

He slayeth, he wasteth, he spouteth his fires

On babes at the bosom, and bed-rid sires;

He bursteth pale cities, through smoke and through
     yell,

And bringeth behind him, hot-blooded, his hell.

Then the weak door is barr'd, and the soul all sore,
And hand-wringing helplessness paceth the floor,
And the lover is slain, and the parents are nigh —

Oh God! let me breathe, and look up at thy sky!
Good is as hundreds, evil as one;
Round about goeth the golden sun.

V.

How Captain Sword, in Consequence of his Great
Victories, became infirm in his Wits.

But to win at the game, whose moves are death,
It maketh a man draw too proud a breath:
And to see his force taken for reason and right,
It tendeth to unsettle his reason quite.
Never did chief of the line of Sword
Keep his wits whole at that drunken board.
He taketh the size, and the roar, and fate,
Of the field of his action, for soul as great:
He smiteth and stunneth the cheek of mankind,
And saith " Lo! I rule both body and mind."

Captain Sword forgot his own soul,

Which of aught save itself, resented controul;

Which whatever his deeds, ordained them still,

Bodiless monarch, enthron'd in his will:

He forgot the close thought, and the burning heart,

And pray'rs, and the mild moon hanging apart,

Which lifteth the seas with her gentle looks,

And growth, and death, and immortal books,

And the Infinite Mildness, the soul of souls,

Which layeth earth soft 'twixt her silver poles;

Which ruleth the stars, and saith not a word;

Whose speed in the hair of no comet is heard;

Which sendeth the soft sun, day by day,

Mighty, and genial, and just alway,

Owning no difference, doing no wrong,

Loving the orbs and the least bird's song,

The great, sweet, warm angel, with golden rod,
Bright with the smile of the distance of God.

   Captain Sword, like a witless thing,
Of all under heaven must needs be king,
King of kings, and lord of lords,
Swayer of souls as well as of swords,
Ruler of speech, and through speech, of thought;
And hence to his brain was a madness brought.
He madden'd in East, he madden'd in West,
Fiercer for sights of men's unrest,
Fiercer for talk, amongst awful men,
Of their new mighty leader, Captain Pen,
A conqueror strange, who sat in his home
Like the wizard that plagued the ships of Rome,
Noiseless, show-less, dealing no death,
But victories, winged, went forth from his breath.

Three thousand miles across the waves *
Did Captain Sword cry, bidding souls be slaves:
Three thousand miles did the echo return
With a laugh and a blow made his old cheeks burn.

Then he call'd to a wrong-maddened people, and
    swore †
Their name in the map should never be more:
Dire came the laugh, and smote worse than before.
Were earthquake a giant, up-thrusting his head
And o'erlooking the nations, not worse were the
    dread.

Then, lo! was a wonder, and sadness to see;
For with that very people, their leader, stood he,

* The American War.   † The French War.

Incarnate afresh, like a Cæsar of old;*
But because he look'd back, and his heart was cold,
Time, hope, and himself for a tale he sold.
Oh largest occasion, by man ever lost!
Oh throne of the world, to the war-dogs tost!

He vanish'd; and thinly there stood in his place
The new shape of Sword, with an humbler face,†
Rebuking his brother, and preaching for right,
Yet aye when it came, standing proud on his might,
And squaring its claims with his old small sight;
Then struck up his drums, with ensign furl'd,
And said, " I will walk through a subject world:
Earth, just as it is, shall for ever endure,

* Napoleon.
† The Duke of Wellington, or existing Military Toryism.

The rich be too rich, and the poor too poor;
And for this I'll stop knowledge. I'll say to it, ' Flow
Thus far; but presume no farther to flow :
For me, as I list, shall the free airs blow.' "

Laugh'd after him loudly that land so fair,*
" The king thou set'st over us, by a free air
Is swept away, senseless." And old Sword then
First knew the might of great Captain Pen.
So strangely it bow'd him, so wilder'd his brain,
That now he stood, hatless, renouncing his reign;
Now mutter'd of dust laid in blood; and now
'Twixt wonder and patience went lifting his brow.
Then suddenly came he, with gowned men,
And said, " Now observe me — *I'm* Captain Pen:

* The Glorious Three Days.

THEN SUDDENLY CAME HE WITH GOWNED MEN,
AND SAID, "NOW OBSERVE ME—I'M CAPTAIN PEN."

Canto V. *p.* 34.

I'll lead all your changes — I'll write all your books —
I'm every thing — all things — I'm clergymen, cooks,
Clerks, carpenters, hosiers — I'm Pitt — I'm Lord Grey."

   'Twas painful to see his extravagant way;
But heart ne'er so bold, and hand ne'er so strong,
What are they, when truth and the wits go wrong?

VI.

Of Captain Pen, and how he fought with Captain Sword.

  Now tidings of Captain Sword and his state
Were brought to the ears of Pen the Great,
Who rose and said, " His time is come."
And he sent him, but not by sound of drum,
Nor trumpet, nor other hasty breath,
Hot with questions of life and death,
But only a letter calm and mild;
And Captain Sword he read it, and smil'd,

And said, half in scorn, and nothing in fear,
(Though his wits seem'd restor'd by a danger near,
For brave was he ever) " Let Captain Pen
Bring at his back a million men,
And I'll talk with his wisdom, and not till then."
Then replied to his messenger Captain Pen,
" I'll bring at my back a *world* of men."

Out laugh'd the captains of Captain Sword,
But their chief look'd vex'd, and said not a word,
For thought and trouble had touch'd his ears
Beyond the bullet-like sense of theirs,
And wherever he went, he was 'ware of a sound
Now heard in the distance, now gathering round,
Which irk'd him to know what the issue might be ;
But the soul of the cause of it well guess'd he.

Indestructible souls among men
Were the souls of the line of Captain Pen;
Sages, patriots, martyrs mild,
Going to the stake, as child
Goeth with his prayer to bed;
Dungeon-beams, from quenchless head;
Poets, making earth aware
Of its wealth in good and fair;
And the benders to their intent,
Of metal and of element;
Of flame the enlightener, beauteous,
And steam, that bursteth his iron house;
And adamantine giants blind,
That, without master, have no mind.

Heir to these, and all their store,
Was Pen, the power unknown of yore;

And as their might still created might,

And each work'd for him by day and by night,

In wealth and wondrous means he grew,

Fit to move the earth anew;

Till his fame began to speak

Pause, as when the thunders wake,

Muttering, in the beds of heaven:

Then, to set the globe more even,

Water he call'd, and Fire, and Haste,

Which hath left old Time displac'd —

And Iron, mightiest now for Pen,

Each of his steps like an army of men —

(Sword little knew what was leaving him then)

And out of the witchcraft of their skill,

A creature he call'd, to wait on his will —

Half iron, half vapour, a dread to behold —

Which evermore panted and evermore roll'd,

And uttered his words a million fold.
Forth sprang they in air, down raining like dew,
And men fed upon them, and mighty they grew.

Ears giddy with custom that sound might not hear,
But it woke up the rest, like an earthquake near;
And that same night of the letter, some strange
Compulsion of soul brought a sense of change;
And at midnight the sound grew into a roll
As the sound of all gath'rings from pole to pole,
From pole unto pole, and from clime to clime,
Like the roll of the wheels of the coming of time;—
A sound as of cities, and sound as of swords
Sharpening, and solemn and terrible words,
And laughter as solemn, and thunderous drumming,
A tread as if all the world were coming.

And then was a lull, and soft voices sweet
Call'd into music those terrible feet,
Which rising on wings, lo! the earth went round
To the burn of their speed with a golden sound;
With a golden sound, and a swift repose,
Such as the blood in the young heart knows;
Such as Love knows, when his tumults cease;
When all is quick, and yet all is at peace.

And when Captain Sword got up next morn,
Lo! a new-fac'd world was born;
For not an anger nor pride would it shew,
Nor aught of the loftiness now found low,
Nor would his own men strike a single blow:
Not a blow for their old, unconsidering lord
Would strike the good soldiers of Captain Sword;

But weaponless all, and wise they stood,
In the level dawn, and calm brotherly good;
Yet bowed to him they, and kiss'd his hands,
For such were their new lord's commands,
Lessons rather, and brotherly plea;
Reverence the past, quoth he;
Reverence the struggle and mystery,
And faces human in their pain;
Nor his the least, that could sustain
Cares of mighty wars, and guide
Calmly where the red deaths ride.

 " But how! what now?" cried Captain Sword;
" Not a blow for your gen'ral? not even a word?
What! traitors? deserters?"

"Ah no!" cried they;
"But the 'game's' at an end; the 'wise' wont play."

"And where's your old spirit?"

"The same, though another;
Man may be strong without maiming his brother."

"But enemies?"

"Enemies! Whence should they come,
When all interchange what was known but to
some?"

"But famine? but plague? worse evils by far."

"O last mighty rhet'ric to charm us to war!

AND SO, LIKE THE TOOL OF A DISUS'D ART,
HE STOOD AT HIS WALL, AND RUSTED APART.

Canto VI. *p.* 44.

Look round—what has earth, now it equably speeds,
To do with these foul and calamitous needs?
Now it equably speeds, and thoughtfully glows,
And its heart is open, never to close?

"Still I can govern," said Captain Sword;
"Fate I respect; and I stick to my word."
And in truth so he did; but the word was one
He had sworn to all vanities under the sun,
To do, for their conq'rors, the least could be done.
Besides, what had *he* with his worn-out story,
To do with the cause he had wrong'd, and the glory?

No: Captain Sword a sword was still,
He could not unteach his lordly will;
He could not attemper his single thought;
It might not be bent, nor newly wrought:

And so, like the tool of a disus'd art,
He stood at his wall, and rusted apart.

'Twas only for many-soul'd Captain Pen
To make a world of swordless men.

POSTSCRIPT;

CONTAINING SOME REMARKS

ON WAR AND MILITARY STATESMEN.

POSTSCRIPT;

CONTAINING SOME REMARKS

ON WAR AND MILITARY STATESMEN.

THE object of this poem is to show the horrors of war, the false ideas of power produced in the minds of its leaders, and, by inference, the unfitness of those leaders for the government of the world.

The author intends no more offence to any one than can be helped: he feels due admiration for that courage and energy, the supposed

E

misdirection of which it deplores; he heartily
acknowledges the probability, that that supposed
misdirection has been hitherto no misdirection,
but a necessity—but he believes that the time
is come when, by encouraging the disposition to
question it, its services and its sufferings may be
no longer required, and he would fain tear asun-
der the veil from the sore places of war,—would
show what has been hitherto kept concealed, or
not shown earnestly, and for the purpose,—would
prove, at all events, that the time has come for
putting an end to those phrases in the narratives
of warfare, by which a suspicious delicacy is
palmed upon the reader, who is told, after every-
thing has been done to excite his admiration of
war, that his feelings are " spared " a recital of
its miseries — that " a veil " is drawn over them
— a " truce " given to descriptions which only
" harrow up the soul," &c.

Suppose it be necessary to "harrow up the soul," in order that the soul be no longer harrowed? Moralists and preachers do not deal after this tender fashion with moral, or even physical consequences, resulting from other evils. Why should they spare these? Why refuse to look their own effeminacy in the face,—their own gaudy and overweening encouragement of what they dare not contemplate in its results? Is a murder in the streets worth attending to,—a single wounded man worth carrying to the hospital,— and are all the murders, and massacres, and fields of wounded, and the madness, the conflagrations, the famines, the miseries of families, and the rickety frames and melancholy bloods of posterity, only fit to have an embroidered handkerchief thrown over them? Must " ladies and gentlemen " be called off, that they may not " look that way," the " sight is so shocking "? Does it become

us to let others endure, what we cannot bear
even to think of ?

Even if nothing else were to come of in-
quiries into the horrors of war, surely they would
cry aloud for some better provision against their
extremity *after* battle,—for some regulated and
certain assistance to the wounded and agonized,—
so that we might hear no longer of men left
in cold and misery all night, writhing with tor-
ture, — of bodies stripped by prowlers, perhaps
murderers, — and of frenzied men, the other
day the darlings of their friends, dying, two and
even several days after the battle, of famine !
The field of Waterloo was not completely cleared
of its dead and dying till nearly a week ! Surely
large companies of men should be organized for
the sole purpose of assisting and clearing away the
field after battle.   They should be steady men,

not lightly admitted, nor unpossessed of some knowledge of surgery, and they should be attached to the surgeon's staff. Both sides would respect them for their office, and keep them sacred from violence. Their duties would be too painful and useful to get them disrespected for not joining in the fight—and possibly, before long, they would help to do away their own necessity, by detailing what they beheld. Is that the reason why there is no such establishment? The question is asked, not in bitterness, but to suggest a self-interrogation to the instincts of war.

I have not thought proper to put notes to the poem, detailing the horrors which I have touched upon; nor even to quote my authorities, which are unfortunately too numerous, and contain worse horrors still. They are furnished by almost every history of a campaign, in all quarters of the world. Circumstances so painful, in a first attempt to

render them public for their own sakes, would,
I thought, even meet with less attention in prose
than in verse, however less fitted they may ap-
pear for it at first sight.   Verse, if it has any
enthusiasm, at once demands and conciliates at-
tention; it proposes to say much in little; and
it associates with it the idea of something con-
solatory, or otherwise sustaining.   But there is
one prose specimen of these details, which I will
give, because it made so great an impression on
me in my youth, that I never afterwards could
help calling it to mind when war was spoken of;
and as I had a good deal to say on that subject,
having been a public journalist during one of the
most interesting periods of modern history, and
never having been blinded into an admiration
of war by the dazzle of victory, the circum-
stance may help to show how salutary a record
of this kind may be, and what an impres-
sion the subject might be brought to make on

society. The passage is in a note to one of
Mr Southey's poems, the " Ode to Horror,"
and is introduced by another frightful record,
less horrible, because there is not such agony
implied in it, nor is it alive.

" I extract " (says Mr Southey) " the following
picture of consummate horror from notes to a
poem written in twelve-syllable verse, upon the
campaign of 1794 and 1795 : it was during the
retreat to Deventer. ' We could not proceed a
hundred yards without perceiving the dead bodies
of men, women, children, and horses, in every
direction. One scene made an impression upon
my memory which time will never be able to
efface. Near another cart we perceived a stout-
looking man and a beautiful young woman, with
an infant, about seven months old, at the breast,
all three frozen and dead. The mother had most

certainly expired in the act of suckling her child; as with one breast exposed she lay upon the drifted snow, the milk to all appearance in a stream drawn from the nipple by the babe, and instantly congealed. The infant seemed as if its lips had but just then been disengaged, and it reposed its little head upon the mother's bosom, with an overflow of milk, frozen as it trickled from the mouth. Their countenances were perfectly composed and fresh, resembling those of persons in a sound and tranquil slumber.'"

" The following description (he continues) of a field of battle is in the words of one who passed over the field of Jemappe, after Doumourier's victory : ' It was on the third day after the victory obtained by general Doumourier over the Austrians, that I rode across the field of battle. The scene lies on a waste common, rendered then more dreary by the desertion of the miserable hovels before occupied by peasants. Everything that resembled a human habitation was desolated, and for the most part they had been burnt or pulled down, to prevent their affording shelter to the posts of the contending armies. The ground was ploughed up by the wheels of the artillery and waggons; everything like herbage was trodden into mire; broken carriages, arms, accoutrements, dead horses and men, were strewed over the heath. *This was the third day after the battle: it was the beginning of November, and for three days a bleak wind and heavy rain had continued incessantly.* There were still remaining alive several hundreds of horses, and of the human victims of that dreadful fight. I can speak with certainty of having seen more than four hundred men *still living*, unsheltered, *without food*, and without any human assistance, most of them confined to the spot where they had fallen *by broken limbs*. The two armies had proceeded, and abandoned these miserable wretches to their fate. *Some of the dead persons appeared to have expired in the act of embracing each other.* Two young French officers, who were brothers, had crawled under the side of a dead horse, where they had contrived a kind of shelter by means of a cloak: they were both mortally wounded, and groaning *for each other.* One very fine young man had just strength enough to drag himself out of a hollow partly filled with water, and was laid upon a little hillock groaning with agony; A GRAPE-SHOT HAD CUT ACROSS THE UPPER PART OF HIS BELLY, AND HE WAS KEEPING IN HIS BOWELS WITH A HANDKERCHIEF AND HAT. He begged of me to end his misery! He complained of dreadful thirst. I filled him the hat of a dead soldier with water, which he nearly drank off at once, and left him to that end of his wretchedness which could not be far distant.' "

" I hope (concludes Mr Southey), I have always felt and expressed an honest and Christian abhorrence of wars, and of the systems that produce them; but my ideas of their immediate horrors fell infinitely short of this authentic picture."

Mr Southey, in his subsequent lives of conquerors, and his other writings, will hardly be thought to have acted up to this "abhorrence of wars, and of the systems that produce them." Nor is he to be blamed for qualifying his view of the subject, equally blameless (surely) as they are to be held who have retained their old views, especially by him who helped to impress them. His friend Mr Wordsworth, in the vivacity of his admonitions to hasty complaints of evil, has gone so far as to say that "Carnage is God's daughter," and thereby subjected himself to the

scoffs of a late noble wit.   He is addressing the
Deity himself :—

> " But thy most dreaded instrument,
>   In working out a pure intent,
>   Is man, array'd for mutual slaughter :
>   Yea, Carnage is thy daughter."

Mr Wordsworth is a great poet and a philosophical
thinker, in spite of his having here paid a tremen-
dous compliment to a rhyme (for unquestionably
the word " slaughter" provoked him into that
imperative " Yea," and its subsequent venturous
affiliation) ; but the judgment, to say no more of
it, is rash.   Whatever the Divine Being intends,
by his permission or use of evil, it becomes us to
think the best of it ; but not to affirm the appro-
priation of the particulars to him under their worst
appellation, seeing that he has implanted in us
a horror of them, and a wish to do them away.
What it is right in him to do, is one thing ;

what it is proper in us to affirm that he actually does, is another. And, above all, it is idle to affirm what he intends to do for ever, and to have us eternally venerate and abstain from questioning an evil. All good and evil, and vice and virtue themselves, might become confounded in the human mind by a like daring; and humanity sit down under every buffet of misfortune, without attempting to resist it: which, fortunately, is impossible. Plato cut this knotty point better, by regarding evil as a thing senseless and unmalignant (indeed no philosopher regards anything as malignant, or malignant for malignity's sake); out of which, or notwithstanding it, good is worked, and to be worked, perhaps, finally to the abolition of evil. But whether this consummation be possible or not, and even if the dark horrors of evil be necessary towards the enjoyment of the light of good, still the horror must be maintained, where the object is really horrible; otherwise, we but the more idly resist the contrast, if necessary—and, what is worse, endanger the chance of melioration, if possible.

Did war appear to me an inevitable evil, I should be one of the last men to shew it in any other than its holiday clothes. I can appeal to writings before the public, to testify whether I am in the habit of making the worst of anything, or of not making it yield its utmost amount of good. My inclinations, as well as my reason, lie all that way. I am a passionate and grateful lover of all the beauties of the universe, moral and material; and the chief business of my life is to endeavour to give others the like fortunate affection. But, on the same principle, I feel it my duty to look evil in the face, in order to discover if it be capable of amendment; and I do not see why the miseries of war are to be spared this interrogation, simply because they are frightful and enormous. Men

get rid of smaller evils which lie in their way—
nay, of great ones ; and there appears to be no
reason why they should not get rid of the greatest,
if they will but have the courage. We have
abolished inquisitions and the rack, burnings foɪ
religion, burnings for witchcraft, hangings for for-
gery (a great triumph in a commercial country),
much of the punishment of death in some coun-
tries, all of it in others. Why not abolish war ?
Mr Wordsworth writes no odes to tell us that the
Inquisition was God's daughter ; though Lope de
Vega, who was one of its officers, might have done
so—and Mr Wordsworth too, had he lived under its
dispensation. Lope de Vega, like Mr Wordsworth
and Mr Southey, was a good man, as well as a ce-
lebrated poet : and we will concede to his memory
what the English poets will, perhaps, not be equally
disposed to grant (for they are severe on the Romish
faith) that even the Inquisition, *like War*, might
possibly have had some utility in its evil, were it

no other than a hastening of Christianity by its
startling contradictions of it. Yet it has gone.
The Inquisition, as War may be hereafter, is no
more. Daughter if it was of the Supreme Good,
it was no immortal daughter. Why should
" Carnage" be,—especially as God has put it in
our heads to get rid of it ?

I am aware of what may be said on these occa-
sions, to "puzzle the will;" and I concede of course,
that mankind may entertain false views of their
power to change anything for the better. I con-
cede, that all change may be only in appearance,
and not make any real difference in the general
amount of good and evil; that evil, to a certain
invariable amount, may be necessary to the amount
of good (the overbalance of which, with a most
hearty and loving sincerity, I ever acknowledge);
and finally, that all which the wisest of men could
utter on any such subject, might possibly be

nothing but a jargon,—the witless and puny voice of what we take to be a mighty orb, but which, after all, is only a particle in the starry dust of the universe.

On the other hand, all this may be something very different from what we take it to be, setting aside even the opinions which consider mind as everything, and time and space themselves as only modifications of it, or breathing-room in which it exists, weaving the thoughts which it calls life, death, and materiality.

But be his metaphysical opinions what they may, who but some fantastic individual, or ultra-contemplative scholar, ever thinks of subjecting to them his practical notions of bettering his condition ! And how soon is it likely that men will leave off endeavouring to secure themselves against the uneasier chances of vicissitude, even if

F

Providence ordains them to do so for no other
end than the preservation of vicissitude itself,
and not in order to help them out of the husks
and thorns of action into the flowers of it, and
into the air of heaven? Certain it is, at all
events, that the human being is incited to increase
his amount of good: and that when he is en-
deavouring to do so, he is at least not fulfilling
the worst part of his necessity. Nobody tells
us, when we attempt to put out a fire and to
save the lives of our neighbours, that Conflagration
is God's daughter, or Murder God's daughter.
On the contrary, these are things which Chris-
tendom is taught to think ill off, and to wish
to put down; and therefore we should put
down war, which is murder and conflagration by
millions.

To those who tell us that nations would grow
cowardly and effeminate without war, we answer,

" Try a reasonable condition of peace first, and then prove it. Try a state of things which mankind have never yet attained, because they had no press, and no universal comparison of notes; and consider, in the meanwhile, whether so cheerful, and intelligent, and just a state, seeing fair play between body and mind, and educated into habits of activity, would be likely to uneducate itself into what was neither respected nor customary. Prove, in the meanwhile, that nations are cowardly and effeminate, that have been long unaccustomed to war; that the South Americans are so; or that all our robust countrymen, who do not " go for soldiers," are timid agriculturists and manufacturers, with not a quoit to throw on the green, or a saucy word to give to an insult. Moral courage is in self-respect and the sense of duty; physical courage is a matter of health or organization. Are these predispositions likely to fail in a community of instructed freemen?

Doubters of advancement are always arguing from a limited past to an unlimited future; that is to say, from a past of which they know but a point, to a future of which they know nothing. They stand on the bridge " between two eternities," seeing a little bit of it behind them, and nothing at all of what is before; and uttering those words unfit for mortal tongue, " man ever was" and " man ever will be." They might as well say what is beyond the stars. It appears to be a part of the necessity of things, from what we see of the improvements they make, that all human improvement should proceed by the co-operation of human means. But what blinker into the night of next week,—what luckless prophet of the impossibilities of steam-boats and steam-carriages, — shall presume to say how far those improvements are to extend? Let no man faint in the co-operation with which God has honoured him.

As to those superabundances of population which wars and other evils are supposed to be necessary in order to keep down, there are questions which have a right to be put, long before any such necessity is assumed: and till those questions be answered, and the experiments dependent upon them tried, the interrogators have a right to assume that no such necessity exists. I do not enter upon them—for I am not bound to do so; but I have touched upon them in the poem; and the " too rich," and other disingenuous half-reasoners, know well what they are. All passionate remedies for evil are themselves evil, and tend to re-produce what they remedy. It is high time for the world to show that it has come to man's estate, and can put down what is wrong without violence. Should the wrong still return, we should have a right to say with the Apostle, " Sufficient unto the day is the evil thereof; " for meanwhile we should " not have done evil that good may come." That " good " may come ! nay, that evil may be perpetuated; for what good, superior to the alternatives denounced, is achieved by this eternal round of war and its causes? Let us do good in a good and kind manner, and trust to the co-operation of Providence for the result. It seems the only real way of attaining to the very best of which our earth is capable; and at the very worst, necessity, like the waters, will find its level, and the equity of things be justified.

I firmly believe, that war, or the sending thousands of our fellow-creatures to cut one another to bits, often for what they have no concern in, nor understand, will one day be reckoned far more absurd than if people were to settle an argument over the dinner-table with their knives, —a logic indeed, which was once fashionable in some places during the " good old times." The

world has seen the absurdity of that practice:
why should it not come to years of discretion,
with respect to violence on a larger scale? The
other day, our own country and the United States
agreed to refer a point in dispute to the arbitra-
tion of the king of Holland; a compliment (if
we are to believe the newspapers) of which his
majesty was justly proud. He struck a medal
on the strength of it, which history will show
as a set-off against his less creditable attempts
to force his opinions upon the Belgians. Why
should not every national dispute be referred, in
like manner, to a third party? There is reason
to suppose, that the judgment would stand a good
chance of being impartial; and it would benefit
the character of the judge, and dispose him to
receive judgments of the same kind; till at length
the custom would prevail, like any other custom;
and men be astonished at the customs that pre-
ceded it. In private life, none but school-boys

and the vulgar settle disputes by blows; even duelling is losing its dignity.

Two nations, or most likely two governments, have a dispute; they reason the point backwards and forwards; they cannot determine it; perhaps they do not wish to determine; so, like two carmen in the street, they fight it out; first, however, dressing themselves up to look fine, and pluming themselves on their absurdity; just as if the two carmen were to go and put on their Sunday clothes, and stick a feather in their hat besides, in order to be as dignified and fantastic as possible. They then " go at it," and cover themselves with mud, blood, and glory. Can anything be more ridiculous? Yet, apart from the habit of thinking otherwise, and being drummed into the notion by the very toys of infancy, the similitude is not one atom too ludicrous; no, nor a thousandth part enough so. I am aware that a sarcasm is but a sarcasm, and need not imply any argument; never includes all;—but it acquires a more respectable character when so much is done to keep it out of sight,—when so many questions are begged against it by " pride, pomp, and circumstance," and allegations of necessity.   Similar allegations may be, and are brought forward, by other nations of the world, in behalf of customs which we, for our parts, think very ridiculous, and do our utmost to put down; never referring them, as we refer our own, to the mysterious ordinations of Providence; or, if we do, never hesitating to suppose, that Providence, in moving us to interfere, is varying its ordinations.   Now, all that I would ask of the advocates of war, is to apply the possible justice of this supposition to their own case, for the purpose of thoroughly investigating the question.

But they will exultingly say, perhaps, " Is this a time for investigating the question, when mili-

tary genius, even for civil purposes, has regained
its ascendancy in the person of the Duke of Wel-
lington?   When the world has shown that it
cannot do without him?   When whigs, radicals,
liberals of all sorts, have proved to be but idle
talkers, in comparison with this man of few words
and many deeds?"   I answer, that it remains to
be proved whether the ascendancy be gained or
not; that I have no belief it will be regained;
and that, in the meanwhile, never was time fitter
for questioning the merits of war, and, by infer-
ence, those of its leaders.   The general peaceful-
ness of the world presents a fair opportunity for
laying the foundations of peaceful opinion; and
the alarm of the moment renders the interrogation
desirable for its immediate sake.

The re-appearance of a military administration,
or of an administration *barely civil*, and military at
heart, may not, at first sight, be thought the most

promising one for hastening a just appreciation of war, and the ascendancy of moral over physical strength. But is it, or can it be, lasting? Will it not provoke—is it not now provoking— a re-action still more peremptory against the claims of Toryism, than the state of things which preceded it? Is it anything but a flash of success, still more indicative of expiring life, and caused only by its convulsive efforts?

If it be, this it is easy enough to predict, that Sir Robert Peel, notwithstanding his abilities, and the better ambition which is natural to them, and which struggles in him with an inferior one, impatient of his origin, will turn out to be nothing but a servant of the aristocracy, and (more or less openly) of a barrack-master. He will be the servant, not of the King, not of the House of Commons, but of the House of Lords, and (as long as such influence lasts, which can be but a

short while), of its military leader. He will do
nothing whatsoever contrary to their dictation,
upon peril of being treated worse than Canning;
and all the reform which he is permitted to
bring about will be only just as much as will
serve to keep off the spirit of it as long as pos-
sible, and to continue the people in that state of
comparative ignorance, which is the only safe-
guard of monopoly. Every unwilling step of
reform will be accompanied with some retrograde
or bye effort in favour of the abuses reformed:
cunning occasion will be seized to convert boons,
demanded by the age, into gifts of party favour,
and bribes for the toleration of what is with-
held; and as knowledge proceeds to extort public
education (for extort it it will, and in its own
way too at last), mark, and see what attempts
will be made to turn knowledge against itself,
and to catechise the nation back into the school-
boy acquiescence of the good people of Germany.

Much good is there in that people—I would not be thought to undervalue it— much *bonhommie*— and in the most despotic districts, as much sensual comfort as can make any people happy who know no other happiness. But England and France, the leaders of Europe, the peregrinators of the world, cannot be confined to those lazy and prospectless paths. They have gone through the feudal reign; they must now go through the commercial (God forbid that for any body's sake they should stop there!), and they will continue to advance, till all are instructed, and all are masters; and government, in however gorgeous a shape, be truly their servant. The problem of existing governments is how to prepare for this inevitable period, and to continue to be its masters, by converting themselves frankly and truly into its friends. For my part, as one of the people, I confess I like the colours and shows of feudalism, and would retain as much of them as would adorn nobler things. I would keep the tiger's skin, though the beast be killed; the painted window, though the superstition be laid in the tomb. Nature likes external beauty, and man likes it. It softens the heart, enriches the imagination, and helps to show us that there are other goods in the world besides bare utility. I would fain see the splendours of royalty combined with the cheapness of a republic and the equal knowledge of all classes. Is such a combination impossible? I would exhort the lovers of feudal splendour to be the last men to think so; for a thousand times more impossible will they find its retention under any other circumstances. Their royalties, their educations, their accomplishments of all sorts, must go along with the Press and its irresistible consequences, or they will be set aside like a child in a corner, who has insisted on keeping the toys and books of his brothers to himself.

Now, there is nothing that irritates a just cause so much as a threatening of force; and all impositions of a military chief on a state, where civil directors will, at least, do as well, is a threatening of force, disguise it, or pretend to laugh at it, as its imposers may. This irritation in England will not produce violence. Public opinion is too strong, and the future too secure. But deeply and daily will increase the disgust and the ridicule; and individuals will get laughed at and catechised who cannot easily be sent out of the way as ambassadors, and who might as well preserve their self-respect a little better. To attempt, however quietly, to overawe the advance of improvement, by the aspect of physical force, is as idle as if soldiers were drawn out to suppress the rising of a flood. The flood rises quietly, irresistibly, without violence—it cannot help it—the waters of knowledge are out, and will " cover the earth." Of what use is it to see the representative of

a by-gone influence—a poor individual mortal
(for he is nothing else in the comparison), fretting
and fuming on the shore of this mighty sea, and
playing the part of a Canute reversed,—an antic
really taking his flatterers at their word?

The first thirty-five years of the nineteenth
century have been rich in experiences of the
sure and certain failure of all soldiership and
Toryism to go heartily along in the cause of the
many. There has been the sovereign instance
of Napoleon Bonaparte himself — of the allies
after him — of Charles the Tenth — of Louis
Philippe, albeit a "schoolmaster,"— and lastly,
of this strange and most involuntary Reformer
the Duke of Wellington, who refused to do, under
Canning, or for principle's sake, what he consented
to do when Canning died, for the sake of regain-
ing power, and of keeping it with as few con-
cessions as possible. Canning perished because

Toryism, or the principle of power for its own
sake, to which he had been a servant, could not
bear to acknowledge him as its master.   His
intellect was just great enough (as his birth was
small enough) to render it jealous of him under
that aspect.   There is an instinct in Toryism
which renders pure intellect intolerable to it,
except in some inferior or mechanical shape, or in
the flattery of voluntary servitude.   But, by a
like instinct, it is not so jealous of military
renown.   It is glad of the doubtful amount of
intellect in military genius, and knows it to be
a good ally in the preservation of power, and in
the substitution of noise and show for qualities
fearless of inspection.   Is it an ascendancy of
this kind which the present age requires, or will
permit ?   Do we want a soldier at the head of
us, when there is nobody abroad to fight with ?
when international as well as national questions
can manifestly settle themselves without him ?

G

and when his appearance in the seat of power can indicate nothing but a hankering after those old substitutions of force for argument, or at best of " an authority for a reason," which every step of reform is hoping to do away ? Do we want him to serve in our shops? to preside over our studies ? to cultivate " peace and good will " among nations? wounding no self love—threatening no social ?

There never was a soldier, purely brought up as such—and it is of such only I speak, and not of rare and even then perilous exceptions,— men educated in philosophy like Epaminondas, or in homely household virtues and citizenship like Washington—but there never was a soldier such as I speak of, who did more for the world than was compatible with his confined and arbitrary breeding. I do not speak, of course, with reference to the unprofessional part of his cha-

racter. Circumstances, especially the participa-
tion of dangers and vicissitude, often conspire
with naturally good qualities to render soldiers
the most amiable of men; and nothing is more
delightful to contemplate than an old military
veteran, whose tenderness of heart has survived
the shocks of the rough work it has been tried in,
till twenty miserable sights of war and horror
start up to the imagination as a set-off against
its attractiveness. But, publicly speaking, the
more a soldier succeeds, the more he looks upon
soldiership as something superior to all other
kinds of ascendancy, and qualified to dispense with
them. He always ends in considering the flower
of the art of government as consisting in issuing
" orders," and that of popular duty as comprised
in " obedience." Cities with him are barracks,
and the nation a conquered country. He is at
best but a pioneer of civilization. When he
undertakes to be the civilizer himself, he makes

mistakes that betray him to others, even sup-
posing him self-deceived. Napoleon, though
he was the accidental instrument of a popular
re-action, was one of the educated tools of the
system that provoked it,—an officer brought up at
a Royal Military College; and in spite of his
boasted legislation and his real genius, such he
ever remained. He did as much for his own
aggrandizement as he could, and no more for the
world than he thought compatible with it. The
same military genius which made him as great as
he was, stopped him short of a greater greatness;
because, quick and imposing as he was in acting
the part of a civil ruler, he was in reality a soldier
and nothing else, and by the excess of the soldier's
propensity (aggrandizement by force), he over-
toppled himself, and fell to pieces. Soldiership
appears to have narrowed or hardened the public
spirit of every man who has spent the chief part
of his life in it, who has died at an age which gives

final proofs of its tendency, and whose history
is thoroughly known.   We all know what Crom-
well did to an honest parliament.   Marlborough
ended in being a miser and the tool of his wife.
Even good-natured, heroic Nelson condescended
to become an executioner at Naples.   Frederick
did much for Prussia, as a power; but what be-
came of her as a people, or power either, before
the popular power of France?   Even Washington
seemed not to comprehend those who thought
that negro-slaves ought to be freed.

In the name of common sense then, what do
we want with a soldier who was born and bred
in circumstances the most arbitrary; who never
advocated a liberal measure as long as he could
help it; and who (without meaning to speak
presumptuously, or in one's own person unau-
thorized by opinion) is one of the merest
soldiers, though a great one, that ever existed,—

without genius of any other sort,—with scarcely
a civil public quality either commanding or en-
gaging (as far as the world in general can see),—
and with no more to say for himself than the most
mechanical clerk in office? In what respect is
the Duke of Wellington better fitted to be a par-
liamentary leader, than the Sir Arthur Wellesley
of twenty years back? Or what has re-cast the
habits and character of the Colonel Wellesley of
the East Indies, to give him an unprofessional
consideration for the lives and liberties of his
fellow-creatures?

And yet the Duke of Wellington (it is said)
may, after all, be in earnest in his professions of
reform and advancement. If so, he will be the
most remarkable instance that ever existed, of
the triumph of reason over the habits of a
life, and the experience of mankind. I have
looked for some such man through a very re-

markable period of the world, when an honest declaration to this effect would have set him at the top of mankind, to be worshipped for ever; and I never found the glorious opportunity seized, — not by Napoleon when he came from Elba, — not by the allies when they conquered him, — not by Louis Philippe, though he was educated in adversity. I mean that he has shown himself a prince born, of the most aristocratic kind; and evidently considers himself as nothing but the head of a new dynasty. When the Duke of Wellington had the opportunity of being a reformer, of his own free will, he resisted it as long as he could. He opposed reform up to the last moment of its freedom from his dictation; he declared that ruin would follow it; that the institutions of the country were perfect without it; and that, at the very least, the less of it the better. And for this enmity, even if no other reason existed,—even if his new light were sincere,—the Duke of Wellington ought not to have the *honour* of leading reform. It is just as if a man had been doing all he could to prevent another from entering his own house, and then, when he found that the by-standers would insist on his having free passage, were to turn to them, smiling, and say, " Well, since it must be so, allow me to do the honours of the mansion." Everybody knows what this proposal would be called by the by-standers. And if the way in which greatness is brought up and spoilt gives it a right to a less homely style of rebuke (as I grant it does), still the absurdity of the Duke's claim is not the less evident, nor the air of it less provoking.

I can imagine but two reasons for the remotest possible permission of this glaring anomaly—this government of anti-reforming reformers—this hospital of sick guides for the healthy, supported

by involuntary contributions: first, sheer neces-
sity (which is ludicrous); and second, a facilita-
tion of church reform through the Lords and
the bench of Bishops; the desirableness of which
facilitation appears to be in no proportion to the
compromise it is likely to make with abuses. I
have read, I believe, all the utmost possible things
that can be said in its favour, the articles, for
instance, written by the *Times* newspaper (ad-
mirable, as far as a rotten cause can let them
be, and when not afflicted by some portentous
mystery of personal resentment); and though I
trust I may lay claim to as much willingness
to be convinced, as most men who have suffered
and reflected, I have not seen a single argument
which did not appear to me fully answered by
the above objection alone (about the " honour ");
setting aside the innumerable convincing ones
urged by reasoners on the other side: for
as to any dearth of statesmen in a country like

this, it never existed, nor ever can, till educa-
tion and public spirit have entirely left it. There
have been the same complaints at every change
in the history of administrations; and the crop
has never failed.

Allow me to state here, that any appearance
of personality in this book is involuntary. Public
principles are sometimes incarnate in individual
shapes; and, in attacking them, the individual may
be seemingly attacked, where, to eyes which look
a little closer, there is evidently no such intention.
I have been obliged to identify, in some measure,
the Power of the Sword with several successive
individuals, and with the Duke of Wellington
most, because he is the reigning shape, and in-
cludes all its pretensions. But as an individual
who am nothing, except in connexion with
what I humanly feel, I dare to affirm, that I
have not only the consideration that becomes

me for all human beings, but a flesh and
blood regard for every body; and that I as
truly respect in the Noble Duke the possession of
military science, of a straight-forward sincerity,
and a valour of which no circumstances or years
can diminish the ready firmness, as I doubt the
fitness of a man of his education, habits, and poli-
tical principles, for the guidance of an intellectual
age.

I dislike Toryism, because I think it an unjust,
exacting, and pernicious thing, which tends to
keep the interests of the many in perpetual sub-
jection to those of the few; but far be it from
me, in common modesty, to dislike those who have
been brought up in its principles, and taught to
think them good,—far less such of them as adorn
it by intellectual or moral qualities, and who
justly claim for it, under its best aspect in private
life, that ease and urbanity of behaviour which

implies an acknowledgment of its claims to respect, even where those claims are partly grounded in prejudice. I heartily grant to the privileged classes, that, enjoying in many respects the best educations, they have been conservators of polished manners, and of the other graces of intercourse. My quarrel with them is, that the inferior part of their education induces them to wish to keep these manners and graces to themselves, together with a superabundance, good for nobody, of all other advantages; and that thus, instead of being the preservers of a beautiful and genial flame, good for all, and in due season partakeable by all, they would hoard and make an idolatrous treasure of it, sacred to one class alone, and such as the diffusion of knowledge renders it alike useless and exasperating to endeavour to withhold.

I will conclude this Postscript with quotations from three writers of the present day, who may

be fairly taken to represent the three distinct
classes of the leaders of knowledge, and who
will show what is thought of the feasibility
of putting an end to war,—the Utilitarian, or
those who are all for the tangible and material
—the Metaphysical, or those who recognize, in
addition, the spiritual and imaginative wants of
mankind—and lastly (in no offensive sense), the
Men of the World, whose opinion will have the
greatest weight of all with the incredulous, and
whose speaker is a soldier to boot, and a man
who evidently sees fair play to all the weaknesses
as well as strengths of our nature.

The first quotation is from the venerable Mr
Bentham, a man who certainly lost sight of no
existing or possible phase of society, such as the
ordinary disputants on this subject contemplate.
I venture to think him not thoroughly philosophi-
cal on the point, especially in what he says in

reproach of men educated to think differently from himself. But the passage will show the growth of opinion in a practical and highly influential quarter.

" Nothing can be worse," says Mr Bentham, " than the general feeling on the subject of war. The Church, the State, the ruling few, the subject many, all seem to have combined, in order to patronise vice and crime in their very widest sphere of evil. Dress a man in particular garments, call him by a particular name, and he shall have authority, on divers occasions, to commit every species of offence, to pillage, to murder, to destroy human felicity, and, for so doing, he shall be rewarded.

" Of all that is pernicious in admiration, the admiration of heroes is the most pernicious; and how delusion should have made us admire what virtue should teach us to hate and loathe, is among the saddest evidences of human weakness and folly. The crimes of heroes seem lost in the vastness of the field they occupy. A lively idea of the mischief they do, of the misery they create, seldom penetrates the mind through the delusions with which thoughtlessness and falsehood have surrounded their names and deeds. Is it that the magnitude of the evil is too gigantic for entrance? We read of twenty thousand men killed in a battle, with no other feeling than that 'it was a glorious victory.' Twenty thousand, or ten thousand, what reck we of their sufferings? The hosts who perished are evidence of the completeness of the triumph; and the completeness of the triumph is the measure of merit, and the glory of the conqueror. Our schoolmasters, and the immoral books they so often put into our hands, have inspired us with an affection for heroes; and the hero is more heroic in proportion to the numbers of the slain—add a cypher, not one iota is added to our disapprobation. Four or two figures give us no more sentiment of pain than one figure, while they add marvellously to the grandeur and splendour of the victor. Let us draw forth one individual from those thousands, or tens of thousands,—his leg has been shivered by one ball, his jaw broken by another—he is bathed in his own blood, and that of his fellows —yet he lives, tortured by thirst, fainting, famishing. He is but one of the twenty thousand —one of the actors and sufferers in the scene of the hero's glory—and of the twenty thousand there is scarcely one whose suffering or death will not be the centre of a circle of misery. Look again, admirers of that hero! Is not this wretched-ness? Because it is repeated ten, ten hundred, ten thousand times, is not this wretchedness?

"The period will assuredly arrive, when better

instructed generations will require all the evidence
of history to credit, that, in times deeming them-
selves enlightened, human beings should have
been honoured with public approval, in the very
proportion of the misery they caused, and the
mischiefs they perpetrated. They will call upon
all the testimony which incredulity can require,
to persuade them that, in passed ages, men there
were—men, too, deemed worthy of popular re-
compense—who, for some small pecuniary retri-
bution, hired themselves out to do any deeds of
pillage, devastation, and murder, which might be
demanded of them. And, still more will it shock
their sensibilities to learn, that such men, such
men-destroyers, were marked out as the eminent
and the illustrious—as the worthy of laurels and
monuments—of eloquence and poetry. In that
better and happier epoch, the wise and the good
will be busied in hurling into oblivion, or dragging
forth for exposure to universal ignominy and ob-

loquy, many of the heads we deem *heroic;* while the true fame and the perdurable glories will be gathered around the creators and diffusers of happiness."—*Deontology.*

Our second quotation is from one of the subtilest and most universal thinkers now living — Thomas Carlyle — chiefly known to the public as a German scholar and the friend of Goethe, but deeply respected by other leading intellects of the day, as a man who sees into the utmost recognized possibilities of knowledge. See what he thinks of war, and of the possibility of putting an end to it. We forget whether we got the extract from the *Edinburgh* or the *Foreign Quarterly Review,* having made it sometime back and mislaid the reference; and we take a liberty with him in mentioning his name as the writer, for which his zeal in the cause of mankind will assuredly pardon us.

" The better minds of all countries," observes Mr Carlyle, " begin to understand each other, and, which follows naturally, to love each other and help each other, by whom ultimately all countries in all their proceedings are governed.

" Late in man's history, yet clearly, at length, it becomes manifest to the dullest, that mind is stronger than matter—that mind is the creator and shaper of matter—that not brute force, but only persuasion and faith, is the King of this world. The true poet, who is but an inspired thinker, is still an Orpheus whose lyre tames the savage beasts, and evokes the dead rocks to fashion themselves into palaces and stately inhabited cities. It has been said, and may be repeated, that literature is fast becoming all in all to us—our Church, our Senate, our whole social constitution. The true Pope of Christen-dom is not that feeble old man in Rome, nor is

its autocrat the Napoleon, the Nicholas, with its
half million even of obedient bayonets; such
autocrat is himself but a more cunningly-devised
bayonet and military engine in the hands of a
mightier than he. The true autocrat, or Pope,
is that man, the real or seeming wisest of the last
age; crowned after death; who finds his hierarchy
of gifted authors, his clergy of assiduous jour-
nalists: whose decretals, written, not on parch-
ment, but on the living souls of men, it were
an inversion of the laws of nature to disobey.
In these times of ours, all intellect has fused
itself into literature; literature—printed thought,
is the molten sea and wonder-bearing chaos,
in which mind after mind casts forth its opinion,
its feeling, to be molten into the general mass,
and to be worked there; interest after interest
is engulfed in it, or embarked in it; higher,
higher it rises round all the edifices of existence;
they must all be molten into it, and anew

bodied forth from it, or stand unconsumed among
its fiery surges. Woe to him whose edifice is
not built of true asbest, and on the everlasting
rock, but on the false sand and the drift-wood of
accident, and the paper and parchment of anti-
quated habit! For the power or powers exist
not on our earth that can say to that sea—roll
back, or bid its proud waves be still.

" What form so omnipotent an element will
assume—how long it will welter to and fro as
a wild democracy, a wilder anarchy—what con-
stitution and organization it will fashion for itself,
and for what depends on it in the depths of
time, is a subject for prophetic conjecture, wherein
brightest hope is not unmingled with fearful
apprehensions and awe at the boundless un-
known. The more cheering is this one thing,
which we do see and know—that its tendency
is to a universal European commonweal; that the

wisest in all nations will communicate and co-
operate ; whereby Europe will again have its
true Sacred College and council of Amphictyons ;
wars will become rarer, less inhuman; and in
the course of centuries, such delirious ferocity
in nations, as in individuals it already is, may
be proscribed and become obsolete for ever."

My last and not least conclusive extract (for
it shows the actual hold which these speculations
have taken of the minds of practical men—of men
out in the world, and even of *soldiers*) is from a
book popular among all classes of readers—the
Bubbles from the Brunnens of Nassau, written by
Major Sir Francis Head. What he says of one
country's educating another, by the natural pro-
gress of books and opinion, and of the effect
which this is likely to have upon governments
even as remote and unwilling as Russia, is par-
ticularly worthy of attention.

The author is speaking of some bathers at whom he had been looking, and of a Russian Prince, who lets us into some curious information respecting the leading-strings in which grown gentlemen are kept by despotism :—

" For more than half an hour I had been indolently watching this amphibious scene, when the landlord entering my room said, that the Russian Prince, G———n, wished to speak to me on some business; and the information was scarcely communicated, when I perceived his Highness standing at the threshold of my door.   With the attention due to his rank, I instantly begged he would do me the honour to walk in ; and, after we had sufficiently bowed to each other, and that I had prevailed on my guest to sit down, I gravely requested him, as I stood before him, to be so good as to state in what way I could have the good fortune to render him any service.   The Prince very briefly replied, that he had called upon me, considering that I was the person in the hotel best capable (he politely inclined his head) of informing him by what route it would be most adviseable for him to proceed to London, it being his wish to visit my country.

"In order at once to solve this very simple problem, I silently unfolded and spread out upon the table my map of Europe; and each of us, as we leant over it, placing a forefinger on or near Wiesbaden (our eyes being fixed upon Dover), we remained in this reflecting attitude for some seconds, until the Prince's finger first solemnly began to trace its route. In doing this, I observed that his Highness's hand kept swerving far into the Netherlands, so, gently pulling it by the thumb towards Paris, I used as much force as I thought decorous, to induce it to advance in a straight line; however, finding my efforts ineffectual, I ventured

with respectful astonishment, to ask, ' Why travel
by so uninteresting a route ' ?

" The Prince at once acknowledged that the
route I had recommended would, by visiting Paris,
afford him the greatest pleasure; but he frankly
told me that no Russian, not even a personage of
his rank, could enter that capital, without first ob-
taining a written permission from the Emperor.

" These words were no sooner uttered, than I
felt my fluent civility suddenly begin to coagu-
late; the attention I paid my guest became
forced and unnatural. I was no longer at my
ease; and though I bowed, strained, and endea-
voured to be, if possible, more respectful than
ever, yet I really could hardly prevent my lips
from muttering aloud, that I had sooner die a
homely English peasant than live to be a Russian
prince !—in short, his Highness's words acted upon

my mind like thunder upon beer. And, more-
over, I could almost have sworn that I was an
old lean wolf, contemptuously observing a bald
ring rubbed by the collar, from the neck of a
sleek, well-fed mastiff dog; however, recovering
myself, I managed to give as much information
as it was in my humble power to afford; and
my noble guest then taking his departure, I
returned to my open window, to give vent in
solitude (as I gazed upon the horse bath) to my
own reflection upon the subject.

"Although the petty rule of my life has been
never to trouble myself about what the world
calls 'politics' — (a fine word, by the by, much
easier expressed than understood) — yet, I must
own, I am always happy when I see a nation
enjoying itself, and melancholy when I observe
any large body of people suffering pain or im-
prisonment. But of all sorts of imprisonment,

that of the mind is, to my taste, the most cruel;
and, therefore, when I consider over what immense
dominions the Emperor of Russia presides, and
how he governs, I cannot help sympathizing most
sincerely with those innocent sufferers, who have
the misfortune to be born his subjects; for if a
Russian Prince be not freely permitted to go to
Paris, in what a melancholy state of slavery and
debasement must exist the minds of what we
call the lower classes?

" As a sovereign remedy for this lamentable
political disorder, many very sensible people in
England prescribe, I know, that we ought to
have resource to arms. I must confess, however,
it seems to me that one of the greatest political
errors England could commit would be to declare,
or to join in declaring, war with Russia; in short,
that an appeal to brute force would, at this moment,
be at once most unscientifically to stop an im-

mense moral engine, which, if left to its work, is quite powerful enough, without bloodshed, to gain for humanity, at no expense at all, its object. The individual who is, I conceive, to overthrow the Emperor of Russia — who is to direct his own legions against himself — who is to do what Napoleon had at the head of his great army failed to effect, is the little child, who, lighted by the single wick of a small lamp, sits at this moment perched above the great steam press of the ' Penny Magazine,' feeding it, from morning till night, with blank papers, which, at almost every pulsation of the engine, comes out stamped on both sides with engravings, and with pages of plain, useful, harmless knowledge, which, by making the lower orders acquainted with foreign lands, foreign productions, various states of society, &c., tend practically to inculcate ' Glory to God in the highest, and on earth peace — good will towards men.' It has already been stated, that what proceeds from this press is now greedily devoured by the people of Europe; indeed, even at Berlin, we know it can hardly be reprinted fast enough.

"This child, then, — 'this sweet little cherub that sits up aloft,' — is the only army that an enlightened country like ours should, I humbly think, deign to oppose to one who reigns in darkness—who trembles at day-light, and whose throne rests upon ignorance and despotism. Compare this mild, peaceful intellectual policy, with the dreadful, savage alternative of going to war, and the difference must surely be evident to everyone. In the former case, we calmly enjoy, first of all, the pleasing reflection, that our country is generously imparting to the nations of Europe the blessing she is tranquilly deriving from the purification of civilization to her own mind;—far from wishing to exterminate, we are gradually illuminating the Russian peasant, we are mildly throwing a gleam of light upon the fetters of the Russian Prince; and surely every well-disposed person must see, that if we will only have patience, the result of this noble, temperate conduct, must produce all that reasonable beings can desire."—*Bubbles from the Brunnens of Nassau*, p. 164.

By the ' Penny Magazine,' our author means, of course, not only that excellent publication, but all cheaply-diffused knowledge—all the tranquil and enlightening deeds of " Captain Pen " in general—of whom it is pleasant to see the gallant Major so useful a servant, the more so from his sympathies with rank and the aristocracy. But " Pen" will make it a matter of necessity, by and by, for all ranks to agree with him, in vindication of their own wit and common sense; and when once this necessity is felt, and fasti-

diousness shall find out that it will be considered
"absurd" to lag behind in the career of know-
ledge and the common good, the cause of the
world is secure.

May princes and people alike find it out by
the kindliest means, and without further violence.
May they discover that no one set of human
beings, perhaps no single individual, can be
thoroughly secure and content, or enabled to
work out his case with equal reasonableness,
till all are so, — a subject for reflection, which
contains, we hope, the beneficent reason *why all
are restless*. The solution of the problem is co-
operation—the means of solving it is the Press.
If the Greeks had had a press, we should probably
have heard nothing of the inconsiderate question,
which demands, why they, with all their philo-
sophy, did not alter the world. They had not
the means. They could not command a general

hearing. Neither had Christianity come up, to make men think of one another's wants, as well as of their own accomplishments. Modern times possess those means, and inherit that divine incitement. May every man exert himself accordingly, and show himself a worthy inhabitant of this beautiful and most capable world!

THE END.

LONDON:
Printed by C. and W. REYNELL,
Little Pulteney Street.

P. 112.

2. The more constrained motion of the hand, which is indispensable to the ordinary use of the Metallic Pen, sooner fatigues the writer.

3. The constraint and fatigue induced by the Metallic Pen cause the performance to be much slower.

CORRECTION OF THE DISADVANTAGES OF THE METALLIC PEN,

By Knight's Patent Spring Pen-Holder.

The new PATENT SPRING PEN-HOLDER, while it renders the act of writing itself easier with any pen, LEAVES TO THE METALLIC PEN ALL ITS ADVANTAGES OVER THE QUILL, AND INTIRELY OBVIATES THE DISADVANTAGES. By allowing the length of what may be called the axis of the Pen, or the distance between the nibs and the writer's fingers, to vary according to the pressure made, the hand may descend considerably without making the pen scratch the paper, and rise without causing the pen to leave it. The freedom of motion thus attained produces these effects :—

1. The difficulty of writing with the common Steel Pen at once ceases when the Pen is united with the Patent Spring Holder.
2. The fatigue is prevented.
3. The slowness is replaced by rapidity.

The elasticity of the Holder is regulated by a screw, so that every writer is enabled to adjust it to his own habit or fancy.

The instrument is not in the least complicated, and not liable to be out of order. It may be used with any of the numerous descriptions of Metallic Pens now made. It is not of expensive construction, so that it may be attained at small cost by the thousands of persons who now use Steel Pens.

The Patent Spring Pen-Holder is now issued, in Albata, with plain handles, price 2s. Silver and Gold Pen-Holders, with fancy handles, will be ready for delivery in the course of April.

Booksellers, Stationers, and Jewellers may be supplied wholesale, on application to Mr Knight, 22 Ludgate street, or through the Agents for the Sale of his Publications.

LEIGH HUNT'S LONDON JOURNAL,

Vol. I.

This Periodical Work is published WEEKLY, in Numbers, price THREE HALF-PENCE, and contains Original Essays by the Editor, Analyses of and Extracts from New Books, Romances of Real Life, and a variety of interesting Communications from Correspondents.

Every MONTH a PART is issued, containing Five Numbers, sewed in a Wrapper, price EIGHTPENCE.

The SUPPLEMENTARY NUMBERS in those months which only contain four Wednesdays, are formed of a Work on the STREETS of the METROPOLIS, their MEMORIES and GREAT MEN, giving the historical, literary, and personal associations of the streets and houses in London, with the persons and events connected with them, and forming a History of the Manners and Customs, and the early and present state and appearance of the Metropolis.

*** The LONDON JOURNAL is Published in London by H. Hooper, 13 Pall Mall East; but is supplied to Agents in the Country by C. Knight, 22 Ludgate street.

GALLERY OF PORTRAITS.

The FOURTH VOLUME of this Work is now completed, and each volume may be had, bound in fancy cloth, and lettered, with gilt tops, price One Guinea.

The following is a list of the Portraits and Memoirs contained : Dante, Sir H. Davy, Kosciusko, Flaxman, Copernicus, Milton, James Watt, Turenne, Hon. R. Boyle, Sir I. Newton, Michael Angelo, Molière, C. J. Fox, Bossuet, Lorenzo de Medici, George Buchanan, Sir C. Wren, Corneille, Halley, Sully, N. Poussin, Harvey, Sir J. Banks, Lord Somers, Smeaton, Buffon, Sir Thos.

2. The more constrained motion of the hand, which is indispensable to the ordinary use of the Metallic Pen, sooner fatigues the writer.

3. The constraint and fatigue induced by the Metallic Pen cause the performance to be much slower.

CORRECTION OF THE DISADVANTAGES OF THE METALLIC PEN,
BY KNIGHT'S PATENT SPRING PEN-HOLDER.

The new PATENT SPRING PEN-HOLDER, while it renders the act of writing itself easier with any pen, LEAVES TO THE METALLIC PEN ALL ITS ADVANTAGES OVER THE QUILL, AND INTIRELY OBVIATES THE DISADVANTAGES. By allowing the length of what may be called the axis of the Pen, or the distance between the nibs and the writer's fingers, to vary according to the pressure made, the hand may descend considerably without making the pen scratch the paper, and rise without causing the pen to leave it. The freedom of motion thus attained produces these effects :—

1. The difficulty of writing with the common Steel Pen at once ceases when the Pen is united with the Patent Spring Holder.
2. The fatigue is prevented.
3. The slowness is replaced by rapidity.

The elasticity of the Holder is regulated by a screw, so that every writer is enabled to adjust it to his own habit or fancy.

The instrument is not in the least complicated, and not liable to be out of order. It may be used with any of the numerous descriptions of Metallic Pens now made. It is not of expensive construction, so that it may be attained at small cost by the thousands of persons who now use Steel Pens.

The Patent Spring Pen-Holder is now issued, in Albata, with plain handles, price 2s. Silver and Gold Pen-Holders, with fancy handles, will be ready for delivery in the course of April.

Booksellers, Stationers, and Jewellers may be supplied wholesale, on application to Mr Knight, 22 Ludgate street, or through the Agents for the Sale of his Publications.

COLOPHON

This facsimile of the First Edition of Leigh Hunt's *Captain Sword and Captain Pen,* and Professor Rhodes Dunlap's illuminating essay, were published for the Friends of the University of Iowa Libraries in observance of the 200th anniversary of Leigh Hunt's birth on October 19, 1784.

H. S. Milford's standard edition of Hunt's *Poetical Works,* 1923, includes a collation of the text with that in Hunt's *Poetical Works* of 1844 and in the Third Edition, 1849, and prints in full the extensive notes and introductory material which Hunt added in that year.

The type used in the introductory essay is Century Light II, a modernized "old style" face, which is faintly similar in color, logic, and letter forms to the unidentified face used by C. and W. Reynell, printers of the 1835 First Edition.

Composed by
Annie Graham & Company, Iowa City
Printed and bound by
Colwell/North Central, St. Paul
Book and jacket design by Norman Sage